The World's Greatest
HOTELS

2013 EDITION

The view from a beachside lounge at Jumeirah Vittaveli, in the Maldives.

The World's Greatest
HOTELS

2013 EDITION

Introduction by Nancy Novogrod

TRAVEL+
LEISURE
BOOKS

AMERICAN EXPRESS PUBLISHING CORPORATION
NEW YORK

Travel+Leisure
The World's Greatest Hotels
Eighth Edition

Editor Jennifer Miranda
Consulting Editors Laura Begley Bloom, Irene Edwards, Peter Jon Lindberg
Art Director Phoebe Flynn Rich
Photo Editor Zoey E. Klein
Consulting Photo Editor Elizabeth Boyle
Production Associate David Richey
Editorial Assistant Nate Storey
Reporters Gabriella Fuller, Marguerite A. Suozzi
Copy Editors David Gunderson, Jane Halsey, Edward Karam, Sarah Khan, Libby Sentz
Researchers Kyle Avallone, Sebastian Girner, Pearly Huang, Paola Singer

TRAVEL+LEISURE
Editor-in-Chief Nancy Novogrod
Design Director Sandra Garcia
Executive Editor/Content Strategist Jennifer Barr
Managing Editor Laura Teusink
Associate Managing Editor Patrick Sheehan
Arts/Research Editor Mario R. Mercado
Copy Chief Kathy Roberson
Photo Director Scott Hall
Production Manager Ayad Sinawi

AMERICAN EXPRESS PUBLISHING CORPORATION
President and Chief Executive Officer Ed Kelly
Chief Marketing Officer and President, Digital Media Mark V. Stanich
CFO, SVP, Corporate Development and Operations Paul B. Francis
VP, General Managers Frank Bland, Keith Strohmeier
VP, Books and Products Marshall Corey
Director, Books Programs Bruce Spanier
Senior Marketing Manager, Branded Books Eric Lucie
Associate Marketing Manager Stacy Mallis
Director of Fulfillment and Premium Value Philip Black
Manager of Customer Experience and Product Development Betsy Wilson
Director of Finance Thomas Noonan
Associate Business Manager Uma Mahabir
VP, Operations Tracy Kelliher
Operations Director Anthony White

Cover: The pool area at Oxygen Jungle Villas, in Uvita, Costa Rica. Photographed by Beth Garrabrant.

Back cover, from top: Stonover Farm, in Lenox, Massachusetts; a lounge at Round Hill, in Jamaica; a guest room at Chambres d'Hôtes Hôtel Verhaegen, in Ghent, Belgium. Photographed by Jessica Antola (top); Theo Morrison (middle); Martha Camarillo (bottom).

ISBN 978-1-932624-58-8

Published by American Express Publishing Corporation
1120 Avenue of the Americas
New York, New York 10036

Distributed by Charlesbridge Publishing
85 Main Street, Watertown, Massachusetts 02472

Printed in the U. S. A.

The bar at Palais Namaskar's Espace T restaurant, in Marrakesh, Morocco.

A guest room at
the Washington
School House Hotel,
in Park City, Utah.

Contents

contents

KEY   **$** *Less than $200*   **$$** *$200 to $350*   **$$$** *$350 to $500*   **$$$$** *$500 to $1,000*   **$$$$$** *More than $1,000*

The pool area
at the Siam,
in Bangkok.

contents

A lobby sitting area at the Efendi Hotel, in Acre, Israel.

Introduction

Part of my role as editor-in-chief of *Travel + Leisure* is serving as a travel confessor—for friends and family, of course, but also for T+L readers, who have plenty to say. Most of your "user" comments about hotels exist on the extreme ends of the spectrum, ranging from wild enthusiasm to crushing disappointment. This is hardly a surprise when you consider how intimate and dependent your relationship can be to the places that cater to your basic human needs.

Because we know what we like when we venture out into the world and we've heard loud and clear what pleases you, it is always a pleasure to step back and consider the astounding range of hotels, resorts, inns, and lodges that are contained within 12 months of issues of our magazine.

With this in mind, we bring you the latest edition of *The World's Greatest Hotels:* a selection of the year's best places to stay, curated by T+L's editors and culled from the thousands of extraordinary destinations we've featured. In this eighth annual compendium, you'll find a wide range of properties, from the classic (a Jamaican resort that once served as Grace Kelly's winter getaway) to the cutting-edge (a luxe tower piercing the Dubai skyline); and from the cozy (a Wisconsin retreat reminiscent of the sleep-away camps of childhood summers) to the exotic (a plush safari lodge in a far-flung corner of the Serengeti).

Some of the destinations featured within these pages demand a considerable degree of commitment, both in terms of time and money, but they offer high rewards. Such is the case with Mashpi Lodge, a glass-enclosed refuge in the heart of the Ecuadoran rain forest; Song Saa, a private-island preserve off the coast of southern Cambodia; and the Berkeley River Lodge, a remote outpost in western Australia's untouched Kimberley region. Others, at a less ambitious distance, are no less satisfying for their relative convenience: take, for example, the Castello di Casole, in the Tuscan hillside just 40 miles outside Florence, and the Saint, a stylish haven housed in a landmark building at the edge of New Orleans's storied French Quarter.

Despite the upheavals and uncertainties of our times, it is noteworthy how many iconic properties are undergoing significant renovations. Witness the head-to-toe refurbishment of the elegant Le Bristol, in Paris, among the city's distinguished palace hotels; the glamorous remake of Los Angeles's legendary hideaway for Hollywood movers and shakers, the Hotel Bel-Air; and the modern reinvention of that doyenne of Asian hospitality, the Mandarin Oriental Bangkok.

Where to begin in choosing your next getaway? To help you in your search, we highlight the winners of T+L's annual World's Best Awards as well as the T+L 500, a comprehensive list of the top hotels and resorts as chosen by you, our readers. At the back of this volume, you will find an index and trips directory organizing properties by location and category, from family-friendly to affordable. We hope you'll turn to these resources for advice—and to this book for inspiration—again and again.

Nancy Novogrod EDITOR-IN-CHIEF

A street view of the Wythe Hotel, in Brooklyn, New York.

United States + Canada

Breakfast at
Stonover Farm.
Left: The inn's
main house.

Stonover Farm

A 15-minute walk from the gates of the Tanglewood Music Center brings you to Stonover Farm—which at first seems like the classic Berkshires country inn, complete with willow trees and a duck pond. But the five suites are more Giorgio Armani than Norman Rockwell, and the onetime horse barn now houses contemporary paintings, sculptures, and photography. The 10-acre property is the vision of Suky Werman and her husband, Tom, a former L.A. record producer who helped steer rock acts like Motley Crüe and Twisted Sister to platinum-selling status. These days, Tom's pursuits are of the quieter sort: there's a library stocked with art and travel books and a greenhouse full of garden roses, and each evening he pours wine for guests and cues up some Bill Evans by the fire.

169 Undermountain Rd.; 413/637-9100; stonoverfarm.com. **$$$**

Co-owner
Suky Werman
at the entrance
to the inn's
art gallery.

Kicking back in the lounge area at the Attwater.

NEWPORT, RHODE ISLAND

The Attwater

This isn't your great-grandfather's Newport. The Rhode Island town perpetually linked with preppy yacht clubs and Gilded Age mansions has gotten an injection of youthful energy thanks to the Attwater, a breezy reinvention of a 1910 inn. Known for her unconventional take on New England style, designer Rachel Reider transformed the hotel's lobby with bold ikat drapes and geometric Osborne & Little wallpaper and splashed the 12 guest rooms with nautical blues, lobster reds, and driftwood grays, a nod to the area's sailing heritage. Add in-room iPads, Apple TV, and house-made Oreos courtesy of the all-day café, and you have a getaway fit for a new generation of tastemakers—minus the robber-baron price tag.

22 Liberty St.; 800/392-3717 or 401/846-7444; theattwater.com. **$$**

Muted seaside hues in one of the Attwater's guest rooms.

Falls Village Inn

When fledgling innkeepers Susan Sweetapple and Colin Chambers bought the Falls Village Inn, the 1834 clapboard structure was the town's forlorn Cinderella. Luckily, a fairy godmother was close at hand: celebrated interior designer Bunny Williams, who lived down the road and offered her decorating services free of charge. For the inn's three rooms and two suites, she selected patterned quilts and crisp linen upholstery, lined the entrance hall with old-fashioned coat hooks, and moved walls and doors to accommodate spacious new bathrooms and king beds. The menu in the dining room is also a village affair, with carrot cake baked by a busboy's mother and Friday-night lobsters ferried in by a retired helicopter pilot. The result is a happy marriage of urban sophistication and rural simplicity.

33 Railroad St.; 860/824-0033; thefallsvillageinn.com. **$**

A lazy afternoon at the Conrad's rooftop bar. Left: The hotel's artful lobby.

Conrad

Battery Park City—the residential high-rise enclave in lower Manhattan—may not be the first place that comes to mind as a hotel hub, but the area has proved a fitting choice for the Conrad group and its first New York hotel. Behind the glass façade, 463 streamlined suites tower above a 15-story atrium lobby turned art gallery, where an aluminum-and-cable installation by Venezuelan architect Monica Ponce de Leon and a massive painting by Sol LeWitt hang overhead. The hotel is already luring the suit-and-tie crowd, who gather each morning for the scrambled-egg bruschetta at Atrio. Not everything is so buttoned-up; at the rooftop Loopy Doopy Bar, which overlooks the Hudson River, the blood-orange, lychee, and gin popsicle, served in Prosecco, is the perfect drink to toast a summer sunset.

102 North End Ave.; 800/266-7237 or 212/945-0100; conradnewyork.com. **$$**

NoMad Hotel's library, which doubles as a cocktail lounge.

NoMad Hotel

The surest sign that urban renewal has reached a tipping point? When a long-ignored neighborhood acquires a trendy new name. In this case, the area is NoMad (North of Madison Square Park), and one of the catalysts for its revival is the NoMad Hotel. Set in a 1903 Beaux-Arts building, the property feels like the ancestral home of some raffish, fabulously wealthy bohemian, with burnished interiors by designer Jacques Garcia and an air of unbuttoned privilege. Food and drink take center stage: in a series of intimate dining rooms and lounges, chef Daniel Humm, of Eleven Madison Park, offers rustic riffs on the French-inspired cuisine he's famous for, including whole roasted chicken with foie gras and truffles. Begin the evening with a cocktail at the wood-paneled bar, where the lighting is perfectly calibrated for seduction.

1170 Broadway; 855/796-1505 or 212/796-1500; thenomadhotel.com. **$$**

Brooklyn meets
Baroque in
a Wythe Hotel
guest room.

BROOKLYN, NEW YORK

Wythe Hotel

A 1901 barrel factory now serves as the setting
for the Wythe Hotel, a $34 million social
center that marks Williamsburg's arrival as
the new Establishment. As such, the 72-room
property hits all the right notes. Everything
is adamantly local, from the wallpaper (made in
Brooklyn's Cobble Hill) to the small-batch
booze and house-made granola in the mini-bars.
Furnishings are crafted from salvaged
wood from the original building, and Reynards,
the farm-to-table restaurant, has a menu
that reads like a locavore's manifesto. In a nod
to the neighborhood's roots, several rooms
come with floor-to-ceiling bunk beds—an haute
version of a hipster crash pad.

*80 Wythe Ave.; 718/460-8000;
wythehotel.com.* **$**

Hamptons, New York

During the golden days of summer, monied Manhattanites ditch their urban trappings for Long Island's idyllic South Fork, with its dramatic dunes, shingled windmills, and the rosy light that has drawn artists from Winslow Homer to Jackson Pollock. Lacking your own beach retreat? Here's where to make yourself at home among the low-key seafood shacks and quirky antiques shops in this long-admired coastal getaway.

GARDINERS BAY

3 SHELTER ISLAND

SAG HARBOR

RTE. 114

AMAGANSETT

EAST HAMPTON

2

1

MONTAUK HWY.

BRIDGEHAMPTON

ATLANTIC OCEAN

1 c/o The Maidstone

This sprawling Greek Revival inn has been *the* place to stay in East Hampton for generations. A welcome overhaul gave it an offbeat new name and a Swedish design sensibility; most of the 19 rooms are inspired by famous Scandinavians (Hans Christian Andersen; Edvard Munch). Svenskt Tenn fabrics add a dose of color to the Living Room restaurant, which serves Nordic-tinged American dishes paired with Hamptons-area wines.

207 Main St., East Hampton; 631/324-5006; themaidstone.com. **$$$**

Patterned prints in c/o The Maidstone's lounge.

One of the Inn at Windmill Lane's sunlit suites.

A stretch of surf and sand at Sunset Beach.

② Inn at Windmill Lane

The team behind the Meeting House, one of the hottest restaurants in Amagansett, has now opened the area's most luxurious hotel. The Inn at Windmill Lane is a worthy splurge: not only do the seven tranquil suites have wood-burning fireplaces and spalike bathrooms but each of the property's three cottages also has its own gym and steam room. Soaring cathedral ceilings and a dual shower make spacious suite No. 5 feel twice its size, as do views over a peaceful hydrangea garden. Grab a bike at the reception desk, then hit the beach, a half-mile away, with your very own chaise, umbrella, and cooler, courtesy of the hotel, in tow.

23 Windmill Lane, Amagansett; 631/267-8500; innatwindmilllane.com. **$$$$**

③ Sunset Beach

On bucolic Shelter Island, André Balazs's converted 1960's motel has a vibrant scene and its own brand of rosé—best sipped at the buzzy French restaurant overlooking the Sound. Inside, 20 white-on-white rooms are refreshingly simple, punctuated by cheery pops of orange and yellow and opening onto private decks that face the water. A word to the wise: beach attire is heavy on the glamour here. Stock up on Eres bikinis and K. Jacques sandals at the in-house boutique. At the end of your stay, you can catch the StndAir seaplane for the 45-minute ride back to Manhattan from the cove in front of the hotel.

35 Shore Rd., Shelter Island; 631/749-2001; sunsetbeachli.com. **$$$**

The Red Stag Grill at the Grand Bohemian Hotel.

Grand Bohemian Hotel

Across the road from the entrance to George Vanderbilt's Biltmore Estate—an 1895 mansion synonymous with opulence—the Grand Bohemian takes a maximalist approach to accommodations. The Tudor-style boutique hotel brings to mind a hunting lodge owned by an eccentric art lover with a passion for taxidermy. Mounted deer heads, carved teak columns, and wild boar sculptures fill every nook and cranny. At the hotel's Red Stag Grill, hand-hewn beams and chain-mail curtains set the stage for the menu of chophouse cuts. Guest rooms, however, are relatively restrained, with tufted velvet headboards illuminated by (what else?) antler-entwined lamps.

11 Boston Way; 888/717-8756 or 828/505-2949; bohemianhotelasheville.com. **$$**

St. Regis Bal Harbour Resort

Fireworks lit up the skies above Miami to mark the opening of St. Regis Bal Harbour, the first luxury hotel in an enclave known for high-end shopping. The $700 million, three-tower development isn't shy about trumpeting its star power: celebrity chef Jean-Georges Vongerichten is behind the restaurant, and the Yabu Pushelberg–designed interiors include an eye-catching entrance hall—a dazzling take on a house of mirrors, crowned by rock-crystal chandeliers. In the 243 guest rooms, more reflective surfaces are on hand in the oversize headboards and walk-in closets, and furnishings in understated tones put the emphasis on the ocean views. And if the in-room technology proves overly confusing, one need only seek sanctuary downstairs at the Remède Spa, where the 24-Karat Designer Facial treatment starts with a copper-enriched peel and ends in a sprinkling of gold oil.

A Deluxe room balcony at the St. Regis Bal Harbour.

9703 Collins Ave.; 877/787-3447 or 305/993-3300; stregis.com. **$$$$**

A playful statue
in the lobby
of Lords South
Beach.

MIAMI BEACH

Lords South Beach

A giant polar bear clutching a beach ball takes pride of place in the lobby.
Oversize prints of Elizabeth Taylor as Cleopatra hang above headboards.
The color scheme bounces between bursts of lemon and cerulean.
Is it any wonder that Lords—the first outpost of a new, gay-friendly
hotel brand—is one of the most talked-about properties in town? The
interiors of this Art Deco building in the center of South Beach are
unapologetically exuberant: witness the gold-tiled Cha Cha Rooster Bar,
which channels King Midas. But not everything is so over-the-top.
The daytime vibe around the three pools is surprisingly subdued, and
the 285-square-foot Cabana rooms are quiet havens rather than
party scenes. Come evening, the hotel's informative iPhone app comes
in handy in your quest for Miami's best martini.

1120 Collins Ave.; 877/448-4754 or 305/674-7800;
lordssouthbeach.com. $

Poolside
cabanas at the
SLS Hotel
South Beach.

SLS Hotel South Beach

Call them the new dream team. The SLS Hotel South Beach is the pedigreed product of nightlife impresario Sam Nazarian and Philippe Starck, whose signature vision is brought to life in 140 white-on-white guest rooms in a 1939 Art Deco building; trompe l'oeil walls and fantastic murals lend a touch of whimsy throughout. The star power extends to the penthouse suites, designed by actor and musician Lenny Kravitz. And José Andrés is the force behind the Bazaar, a Spanish-Asian bistro where trendsetters dine on lobster gazpacho and pork-belly *bao*. The scene peaks at Hyde Beach, an 8,000-square-foot poolside lounge that draws the likes of Lebron and D-Wade.

*1701 Collins Ave.; 855/757-7623
or 305/674-1701; slshotels.com.* **$$$**

The Z

On a residential side street near Courthouse Square, the Z feels like a sorority house of sorts in this gracious college town. Its proprietors, sisters Annie and Brittany Zeleskey, graduated from nearby Ole Miss but stuck around to open a tiny inn with statement style. The three bedrooms are decorated with antique furnishings and vintage books; common areas have formal linens and coffee tables laden with eclectic objets d'art. A swing on the front porch is the ideal perch for sipping a glass of iced sun tea and indulging in the decadent treats—from maple-frosted cinnamon rolls to s'mores pie—that the Zeleskeys bake each day. The sisters can also point you to the best tailgate parties during football season and the finest fried catfish in the Delta.

1405 Pierce Ave.; 713/927-1295; thez-oxford.com. **$**

Timeworn
accents in one
of the Z's sunny
guest rooms.

House-made sweet-potato doughnuts from the Saint Hotel's restaurant. Above: A single king room.

The Saint Hotel

On a lively edge of the French Quarter, the Saint is a crisp, highly stylized fantasia. Owner D. Mark Wyant, an American Airlines pilot, and his mother restored the landmark 1909 Audubon Building on Canal Street, preserving the Beaux-Arts façade while adding fanciful touches to interiors. Stark white columns and sheer drapes line the lobby, leading to a custom-made pool table below a bell-shaped chandelier. In the 166 rooms, white lacquered furnishings complement indigo ceilings (a nod to Wyant's day job); downstairs in the Burgundy Bar, sultry red sets the stage for live jazz performances. And in a famously finicky food town, the hotel's restaurant, Tempt, has been embraced by locals. On weekends, the communal table fills with New Orleanians ordering classic Louisiana crab cakes and ice-cold Abita beers.

931 Canal St.; 504/522-5400; thesainthotelneworleans.com. **$$**

The communal
table at the
Saint's Tempt
restaurant.

The Prairie's corrugated-tin Ranger's Lounge.

A farm-fresh breakfast. Right: Vintage accessories in a cottage.

The Prairie

Welcome to the cult of Shabby Chic. After launching a hyper-successful decorating business, multiple retail stores, and a home-accessories line for QVC, design maven Rachel Ashwell decided to create the ultimate expression of her ultrafeminine aesthetic. Enter this seven-bedroom B&B, an 1800's homestead on 46 acres of rolling grassland. Each of the five cottages and cabins is filled with flea market finds: hodgepodge floral prints, mismatched china, and retro furnishings awash in soothing pastel hues. (Even the taxidermied deer wear flowered hats.) Admittedly, organized activities in this area rank low on the agenda, so time your visit around the quarterly antiques fair in tiny Round Top, the source for so many of Ashwell's own impeccably curated treasures.

5808 Wagner Rd.; 979/836-4975; theprairiebyrachelashwell.com. **$$**

Hanging out in one of Wandawega Lake Resort's tree-house cabins.

Wandawega Lake Resort

Summer camp for grown-ups—that's the philosophy behind Wandawega, a 1920's lakeside compound reimagined by a creative young couple. Ninety minutes from Chicago, the rustic retreat summons up a simpler, more carefree era, with billiards and board games instead of TV's, and outdoor activities that range from archery to fishing with antique rods and minnow buckets. Concessions to the modern world include Internet and air-conditioning in the main lodge, but everything else is straight out of a Boy Scouts outing: the swimming hole, the rope swing, the tents and cabins furnished with vintage beds and Coleman lanterns. There are no bathrooms in the suites and no meals unless you make them yourself; you're even asked to bring your own soap. Consider it a heartland vacation, Huck Finn–style.

W5453 Lakeview; no phone; wandawega.com. **$**

Washington School House Hotel

Washington School
House Hotel's
limestone exterior.
Opposite: The
inn's main lounge.

Call it the Sundance effect. Three recent hotel openings—the Waldorf Astoria Park City, St. Regis Deer Valley, and Montage Deer Valley—cemented this ski town's status as a jet-set destination. Now those big names are getting some serious competition from a tiny off-peak gem: the Washington School House, an 1889 limestone elementary school reborn as an elegant inn. More Alpine chic than Rocky Mountain rustic, the 12 rooms have creamy white wainscoting and Gallic and Swedish antiques (gilt wingback chairs; 18th-century tables), as well as oak floors salvaged from a barn near Salt Lake City. Staffers offer spot-on recommendations for restaurants and boutiques and instantly coordinate transportation to your ski trail of choice. Oh, and that famous film festival? It's just steps from the door.

542 Park Ave.; 800/824-1672 or 435/649-3800; washingtonschoolhouse.com. **$$$**

MERCED, CALIFORNIA

Hooper House Bear Creek Inn

As travel destinations go, California's Central Valley—a bucolic farming region with both up-and-coming wineries and mom-and-pop cafés—remains largely overlooked. But the sleepy town of Merced has a few surprises up its sleeve, including the Hooper House Bear Creek Inn. Owned by a fourth-generation farmer, the "White House" is set on one and a half acres shaded by magnolia and citrus trees. Inside, the five light-filled bedrooms have electric fireplaces, sleigh beds, and antique leather furnishings. Be sure to bring a hearty appetite to the breakfast table for innkeeper Rhonda Prothro's generous frittatas and berry-topped parfaits.

575 W. North Bear Creek Dr.; 209/723-3991; hooperhouse.com. **$**

A seating area in the Inn at the Presidio's dining room lounge.

Inn at the Presidio

In a city renowned for its natural beauty, the Inn at the Presidio has a location that trumps all: it's the only hotel in the 1,500-acre Presidio, a military base turned national park with terrain that ranges from forest to beach. The Georgian Revival structure, a former barracks for unmarried officers, invokes its origins with historic mementos that include antique bugles and framed 1900's-era postcards. Most of the 22 guest rooms are actually two-room suites with fireplaces; rocking chairs on the porch provide a cozy place to retreat during chilly nights. Book a room on the top floor for views of the Golden Gate Bridge emerging above the fog.

42 Moraga Ave.; 415/800-7356; innatthepresidio.com. **$**

A guest room at Hotel Bel-Air. Opposite: Sunbathing by the pool.

LOS ANGELES

Hotel Bel-Air

Los Angeles's iconic canyon estate has a bold new look. Gone are the chintz fabrics and needlepoint rugs; designer Alexandra Champalimaud gave the 103 guest rooms a Hollywood Regency–style makeover in a contemporary palette of cream, black, and white. Architect David Rockwell imbued the indoor-outdoor restaurant with a glamorous theatricality, adding banquettes and custom-upholstered director's chairs (the perfect seats for Hollywood's power players). California culinary legend Wolfgang Puck oversaw the menu, reinventing old favorites such as the tortilla soup—here served with grilled chicken and guajillo chiles. Still, classicists shouldn't fret. The babbling fountains and resident swans remain as serene as ever. And the mood is straight out of a Slim Aarons photograph: timeless, tasteful, and without a care in the world.

701 Stone Canyon Rd.; 800/648-4097 or 310/472-1211; hotelbelair.com. **$$$**

Rosario Resort & Spa

There's plenty of natural beauty on display on horseshoe-shaped Orcas, the largest island in the San Juan archipelago. Amid the evergreen forests above Cascade Bay stands Rosario, the former residence of Seattle shipbuilder and mayor Robert Moran. The original 1906 Arts and Crafts mansion now serves as a museum; look for the mahogany-and-teak music room with its turn-of-the-20th-century Steinway grand piano and a two-story Aeolian pipe organ that's still played today. Guest rooms, which are in outlying buildings, are simple and comfortable, keeping the focus on the Puget Sound views. Craving a bird's-eye look at it all? Take a seaplane from Seattle right to Rosario's own marina.

1400 Rosario Rd.; 800/562-8820 or 360/376-2222; rosarioresort.com. $

Rosario Resort & Spa's pool, which overlooks Puget Sound.

Toronto

Thanks to an infusion of fashion-forward shops, inventive restaurants and cocktail lounges, and starchitect-designed feats that are destined to become landmarks, Canada's largest metropolis has gained an edgy style all its own. Now three newcomers to Toronto's hotel scene—each bringing its own brand of big-city sophistication—are making it easier than ever to take it all in.

1 Shangri-La

A huge nature sculpture greets guests at the entrance to this outpost of the Hong Kong–based Shangri-La group. The Asian influence is understated, yet distinct in the 202-room hotel: walls are covered in raw silk and a Japanese garden insulates the building from the urban din. But there's no escaping the buzz from David Chang's Momofuku restaurant, the New York City import whose pork buns and spicy miso ramen have earned it a cult following.

188 University Ave.; 866/565-5050 or 647/788-8888; shangri-la.com. **$$$$**

Inside Shangri-La's Bosk bar.

A sitting area in the lobby of the Trump International Hotel & Tower.

The exterior of the Four Seasons' new flagship.

2 Trump International Hotel & Tower

In the city's financial district, this 900-foot, 65-story glass monolith is about as subtle as the Donald himself, from the hulking 13,000-pound crystal installation in the lobby to the $7 gold bullion–shaped chocolates stocked in the mini-bar. The 261 rooms start at a generous 550 square feet; king-size beds are outfitted in Italian Bellino linens (yes, pillow menus are provided). At the tri-level Quartz Crystal Spa, where treatments are inspired by 19th-century Russian healing baths, the infinity-edge saltwater lap pool is surrounded by skyscraping views.

325 Bay St.; 855/878-6700 or 416/306-5800; trumphotelcollection.com. **$$$**

3 Four Seasons Hotel

The Toronto-based group has reconstructed its hometown flagship, two blocks from the original location, in the city's hip Yorkville neighborhood. The lobby is adorned with dark wood furnishings, but the 259 rooms, designed by Yabu Pushelberg, are simple and light, many with large bay windows that actually open and personal iPads that you can use to book spa treatments or find the next dining hot spot. It happens to be downstairs: at Café Boulud, the superchef riffs on bistro classics (duck terrine; mushroom fricassee), but it's his famous beef-and-pulled-pork burger you'll want to try at the casual D Bar.

60 Yorkville Ave.; 800/332-3442 or 416/964-0411; fourseasons.com. **$$$$**

VANCOUVER

Rosewood Hotel Georgia

Fedora-clad doormen and an ornate, grandfatherly wall clock pay tribute to the past at the Rosewood Hotel Georgia, which originally opened in 1927. And although a $90 million overhaul has given the property a fresh look, the soul of the place remains intact. Rather than trying to compete with the city's gleaming high-rises, the 156-room hotel nurtures the same intimate scale that drew everyone from Elvis Presley to the Beatles. Staff members pride themselves on anticipating your needs even before you realize them. (Reading glasses wiped clean at turndown? Check.) Hometown chef David Hawksworth's namesake restaurant is garnering acclaim for its pristine Pacific seafood—don't miss the pan-roasted sablefish—and the in-house art collection is among the largest private holdings of Canadian art in the country. If you must leave the premises, do so in style—via the on-call chauffeured Bentley. Tell Jim we said hello.

801 W. Georgia St.; 888/767-3966 or 604/682-5566; rosewoodhotels.com. **$$$**

Hawksworth, a restaurant at the Rosewood Hotel Georgia.

Setting up at the Ritz-Carlton's Maison Boulud.

52

Ritz-Carlton

In celebration of its 100th anniversary, the oldest Ritz-Carlton in North America embarked upon a renovation that melded history with high-tech innovations. The four-year, $200 million revamp of the 1912 Beaux-Arts masterpiece retained the original marble-lined fireplaces, coffered ceilings, and sweeping staircase where society swans in ballgowns once made their entrances. But what the hotel truly prides itself on are the energy-saving additions: motion-sensor lighting; thermostats that activate room-temperature preferences upon check-in; a saltwater pool warmed by excess kitchen heat. In the restaurant, Maison Boulud, the sleek cherry wall panels and glass dividers come courtesy of Tokyo design firm Super Potato. Still, some things are better left unchanged— a grand afternoon tea is still served in the finest Ritz-Carlton tradition.

1228 Sherbrooke St.; 800/241-3333 or 514/842-4212; ritzcarlton.com. **$$$**

united states+canada

A cabana terrace as diving board at the Rockhouse Hotel & Spa, in Jamaica.

Caribbean

Jon Baker in the Trident Castle & Hotel's Great Hall.

Trident Castle & Hotel

First there was Geejam, a retreat whose state-of-the-art recording studio made Port Antonio the go-to destination for music industry insiders like Drake and Gwen Stefani. Now, its owner (and onetime record producer) Jon Baker has set his sights on the fashion crowd, partnering with Jamaican-born entrepreneur Michael Lee-Chin to open the Trident Castle & Hotel. A backdrop for countless photo shoots, the quirky former residence—which houses eight bedrooms and 13 freestanding villas—eschews island clichés for something bolder. Its 1979 exterior remains a bit of folly, calling to mind the Hohensalzburg in Austria; a life-size horse with a lampshade on its head greets guests at the door. In keeping with the anything-goes aesthetic, Mike's Supper Club turns out creative Japanese-Jamaican dishes to the tunes of a bright red 1917 grand piano.

Anchovy; 876/633-7000; geejamcollection.com. **$$**

The ocean-facing property, built in 1979.

Round Hill

In the 1960's, Round Hill attracted seemingly every celebrity under the sun (Grace Kelly; Babe Paley; the Kennedys)—and put Jamaica on the tourism map. Today, that gilded legacy lives on. Redesigned in classic tropical style by Ralph Lauren, 36 white-on-white rooms reside in the plantation-like Pineapple House, and 27 villas are scattered among coconut and allspice groves. The 18th-century great house is now a spa that specializes in organic treatments (try the pineapple-and-frangipani exfoliating scrub). In the kitchen, Martin Maginley elevates such Jamaican dishes as jerk chicken and oxtails for one of the best meals on the island. And the boldface names keep coming.

John Pringle Dr.; 800/972-2159; roundhill.com.
$$$$

The living room in one of Round Hill's villa suites.

A prime sunbathing spot at Rockhouse Hotel & Spa.

Rockhouse Hotel & Spa

Though it bears little resemblance to the sealed, all-inclusive compounds elsewhere on Jamaica, there's something about Rockhouse that makes you never want to leave. Could it be the sunset views from the hotel's clifftop perch? Or the thrill of leaping into snorkel-worthy waters each morning, right from your bungalow's door? One more reason to feel good about your stay: the hotel takes community engagement to a whole new level. In 2008, the Rockhouse Foundation funded the renovation of a local library. And in 2012, it completed the makeover of a grammar school in a small fishing village. Guests can visit both sites every Thursday—proof that your travel dollars really do go a long way.

West End Rd.; 876/957-4373; rockhousehotel.com. **$**

caribbean

59

SAN JUAN, PUERTO RICO

Château Cervantes

The restored 18th-century town house that serves as the setting for this sophisticated boutique hotel honors its Spanish heritage in more than just its name (a tribute to the author of *Don Quixote*). Local designer Nono Maldonado emphasized the building's airy, European feel by preserving its high ceilings, arched doorways, and shuttered balconies overlooking the busy street below. But the 12 rooms and suites are luxuriously up-to-date with sleek, earth-toned furnishings, contemporary artwork, and sumptuous linens. Downstairs, Panza (named for Quixote's sidekick, of course) is one of Old San Juan's buzziest restaurants, where a fashionable crowd mingles over cocktails and creative tropical cuisine: a coconut-accented lobster bisque; decadent bread pudding served with guava sorbet. It's the best of New World flavors in the heart of Old San Juan.

329 Recinto Sur; 787/724-7722; cervantespr.com. **$**

The hotel's
original
18th-century
façade.

Karibuni Lodge

In low-key French St. Martin, the hillside Karibuni Lodge calls to mind an exotic—if far less dusty—African safari camp. (Its name comes from the Swahili word for *welcome*.) Six rustic-chic studios incorporate rough concrete walls, Guyanese redwood bookcases, and just the right mix of Caribbean and sub-Saharan objets, from corrugated-metal mirrors to hand-carved wooden elephants. Broad doorways open onto terraces with trees growing straight through them; beyond stretches the beguiling expanse of Cul de Sac Bay, dotted with tiny green islets. Owners Marion and Erick Clement are on hand to ferry you by boat to one of them: nearby Pinel, where you'll find their beachside restaurant Le Karibuni. The place is invariably packed with bronzed day-trippers queuing up for barbecued wahoo and mahimahi. Good thing hotel guests get first dibs on tables.

29 Les Terrasses de Cul de Sac; 590-690/643-858; lekaribuni.com. **$$**

Karibuni Lodge's pool area, overlooking Cul de Sac Bay.

A view of Baie de St.-Jean from Hotel Le Village St. Barth's pool. Right: An in-room rain shower.

Hotel Le Village St. Barth

Long before the glitterati descended and St. Bart's became, well, St. Bart's, the pioneering Charneau family opened Le Village St.-Jean. Forty-four years later, the bayside hotel has a new name and a fresh look that embodies the oft-used phrase "island chic." Bordered by sweet-scented frangipani and palm trees, 30 stone cottages and suites feature high, wood-beamed ceilings and teak furniture; large, airy bathrooms; and colorful paintings by local artists on vibrantly hued walls. There's also a library full of travel classics that the Charneaus have collected over the years. For all the upgrades, Le Village is still among St. Bart's best deals during high season. Use the savings to treat yourself to a deep-tissue massage on your private terrace, looking out across Baie de St.-Jean.

Baie de St.-Jean; 590-590/276-139; villagestjeanhotel.com. **$$**

The Jacuzzi
Suite, with
its vistas of
St. Bart's
forested hills.

The pool at
Hermitage
Plantation Inn.

Hermitage Plantation Inn

For the title of "least touristy Caribbean isle," Nevis may well be the front-runner. Whole stretches of coastline have nary a high-rise hotel in sight. Troops of vervet monkeys skitter along the roads; sulfur springs bubble in remote corners; the rain forest is a riot of colorful flora. The island has become a retreat for the quietly well-to-do—but not every property has only the 1 percent in mind. At the deceptively affordable Hermitage Plantation Inn, the former British colony's roots are evident in the 15 pastel-hued gingerbread cottages, furnished with colonial-era antiques, that are sprinkled among the bougainvillea gardens of a former sugar plantation. They share the grounds with a 350-year-old great house, where full tea is served on a veranda beside groves of mango and hibiscus. In the mood for something stiffer? Don't miss the inn's rum punch—much like Nevis itself, the centuries-old recipe is a closely guarded secret.

Pond Hill; 869/469-3477; hermitagenevis.com. **$$**

Dominica

No wonder this Caribbean destination markets itself as "the nature island." With lush jungles harboring cascading waterfalls, volcanoes shrouded by steam-spewing fumaroles, and charcoal sands that disappear into the waves, Dominica feels like some primordial lost world. At these hotels—which are as easy on the eyes as they are on the environment—you can dive right in without disturbing the peace.

Map labels:
ATLANTIC OCEAN
1
NORTHERN FOREST RESERVE
CENTRAL FOREST RESERVE
2
MORNE TROIS PITONS NATIONAL PARK
ROSEAU
CARIBBEAN SEA
3

1 Secret Bay

Created by Venezuelan architect Fruto Vivas, Secret Bay's four wood-and-glass villas seem to rise from the bush. Each was made using local hardwood to blend with the forested surroundings; floor-to-ceiling windows let in plenty of light. Outdoor showers are ideal for watching the sun dip beyond the azure water, while two secluded beaches and a hidden sea cave—not to mention a cook at your disposal for in-room meals—offer the perfect excuse to stay right where you are.

Tibay, Portsmouth; 767/445-4444; secretbay.dm. $$$

Secret Bay's ocean-facing infinity pool.

The spa at Rosalie Bay Resort.

One of Jungle Bay Resort's treetop guest suites.

2 Rosalie Bay Resort

On 22 verdant acres at the edge of Morne Trois Pitons National Park, among thickets of noni, Rosalie Bay has become one of the few carbon-negative resorts in the world—thanks not only to solar panels but also to its own wind turbine, organic gardens, and a spring-fed swimming pool. The 28 gingerbread-trimmed cottages, which feature carved mahogany furnishings and red-cedar four-poster beds, look out on the beach, the garden, or the Rosalie River. In the plantation-style restaurant, most dishes are made with regional ingredients, from the Kalinago porridge with cassava root to the smoked cod atop fried green plantains.

Rosalie; 767/446-1010; rosaliebay.com. **$$**

3 Jungle Bay Resort & Spa

The Atlantic coastline stretching out from this hilly 55-acre retreat is rugged, green, and isolated. Owner Sam Raphael placed each of the 35 guest quarters—more tree houses than cottages—well apart from its neighbors to minimize erosion. For construction, he hired farmers from the island's failing banana industry, and trained some of them to craft furniture for the guest rooms. The result: an appealingly simple, rough-hewn aesthetic (woven-bamboo fans; white-cedar dressers), complemented by hammocks on every balcony that afford views of the hazy rain forest or the aquamarine sea.

Pointe Mulâtre; 767/446-1789; junglebaydominica.com; all-inclusive. **$$$$**

COOK

Guest rooms
overlooking
Thalemont Bay.
Below: A
pastel bedroom.

MARTINIQUE

Plein Soleil

The pastries are French; the madras fabrics, Indian; the music, rooted in Cuban rumba. But Martinique, the Caribbean's richest melting pot, is pure Creole. The same can be said for Plein Soleil, a tasteful collection of villas facing Thalemont Bay. The 16 muted guest rooms and suites have linen-draped chaise longues worthy of Empress Josephine—a Martinique native— and the open-air restaurant is housed in a 19th-century French-colonial building. The menu, however, is a multicultural mash-up: spicy pork served in a creamy curry sauce shares the spotlight with vegetable soup topped with quail and foie gras. Accommodating staff members will help you arrange everything from in-room ayurvedic massages to fishing tours of the island in a traditional *yole ronde* boat. For the full cultural immersion, hop in the car and head to Fort-de-France's covered market, a heady mix of spices and fruits from the tropics.

Le François; 596-596/380-777; hotelpleinsoleil.fr. **$$**

Buccament Bay Resort

The Bay Beach Club restaurant at Buccament Bay Resort.

A string of 32 islands and cays just south of St. Lucia, St. Vincent and the Grenadines has long been an under-the-radar getaway for the jet set. (A new airport will soon make the region more accessible to travelers. Built on volcanic black sand and set within 37 acres of palm-fringed gardens, the 125 light-filled villas at Buccament Bay Resort beckon with clean lines and contemporary luxuries (free Wi-Fi; private plunge pools). At the on-site sports complex, tennis lessons are led by former Wimbledon singles champion Pat Cash, and the soccer school is run by Britain's Liverpool Football Club. Not the athletic type? Drama buffs can hone their craft with a West End veteran through the hotel's performing arts program. Or you can board the catamaran at sunset for a dolphin-spotting tour nearby—a guaranteed crowd-pleaser.

877/502-2022; buccamentbay.com; all-inclusive; three-night minimum.
$$$$

A view of the restaurant from the pool area.

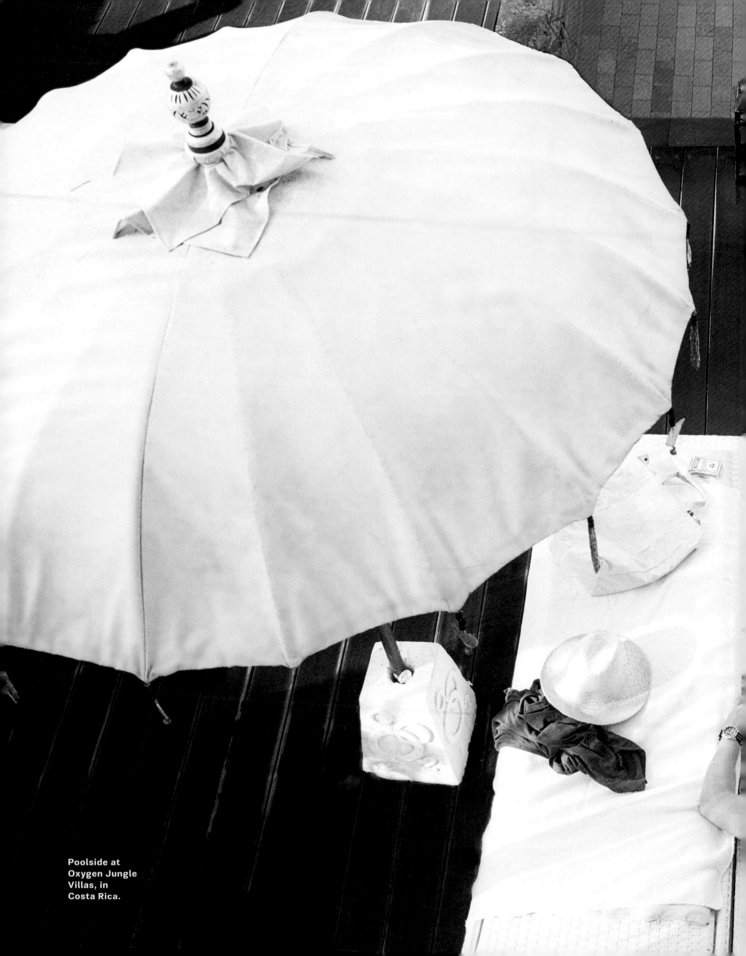

Poolside at
Oxygen Jungle
Villas, in
Costa Rica.

There's no grand driveway—not even a sign—
leading to the revamped Viceroy Riviera Maya,
the latest addition to the brand's portfolio
of sleek hideaways. But that hasn't stopped the
resort formerly known as the Tides from
making a splash. Eleven new villas, with private
plunge pools, outdoor showers, and tubs big
enough for two, start at an ivory-sand beach
and disappear into the jungle; the 30 thatched-
roof casitas have shaded patios where
hammocks provide the ideal perch for observing
scurrying iguanas, trilling birds, and bands of
spider monkeys playing in sapote trees. Near
the casual waterfront restaurant, a chef teaches
classes that specialize in indigenous Mayan
methods. The resort's biggest draw, however,
may be the Wayak Spa; opt for the ancient
herbal cleansing ritual, performed by a native
temazcalera (healer). It's hard to believe
that Playa del Carmen's raucous nightlife is just
15 minutes away.

*Playa Xcalacoco; 800/578-0281 or 52-984/
877-3000; viceroyhotelsandresorts.com.* **$$$$**

**One of the
resort's two pools,
backed by the
Caribbean Sea.**

Endémico Resguardo Silvestre

Hurtling down dusty Route 3, you'd never guess that Baja's arid landscape could be home to one of the Northern Hemisphere's great, undiscovered wine regions. In on the secret: native hotel company Grupo Habita, which set its eco-friendly Endémico Resguardo Silvestre high above the Valle de Guadalupe's boutique vineyards and Mission-style haciendas. Just 40 minutes from Ensenada, the property's 20 mountainside bungalows have minimal impact on the rugged terrain and are sited to catch nightly desert breezes. Mexican architect Jorge Gracia crafted the structures out of steel that changes color and texture over time, further harmonizing them with their surroundings. Next door, you'll find a winery run by a Napa Valley enologist and a Slow Food restaurant overseen by the Culinary Arts School of Tijuana. Sample some of the area's buttery Chardonnays on a private balcony there, or take in the panoramic vistas from your room's terrace as the fire from a clay *chiminea* glows against the dusk.

Km 75, Crta. Tecate-Ensenada; 800/337-4685; designhotels.com. **$**

Tulum, Mexico

On the southern tip of the Riviera Maya, the former hippie outpost of Tulum has become one of the country's most in-vogue destinations. To keep up with increasing demand over the past decade, stylish expats and local craftsmen have transformed the coast into an enclave of chic yet authentic hotels with a decidedly casual vibe. And thanks to scant Internet access and little telephone service, the scene is fashionably low-key.

CANCÚN

QUINTANA
ROO
NATIONAL
PARK

MEXICO 307

TULUM
ARCHAEOLOGICAL
ZONE

3
2
1

CARIBBEAN
SEA

SIAN-KA'AN
BIOSPHERE
RESERVE

1 Be Tulum

Looking for the swankiest digs in town? Each of owner Sebastian Sas's 20 suites at Be Tulum comes with boho-luxe touches like Brazilian wood floors topped with tiger-print rugs and mosaic-tiled private pools. The rooms also have limestone walls, freestanding tubs, and air-conditioning— a rarity in these parts. But the boutique hotel offers something even more ambitious: a holistic card reading that promises to "recess your inner wisdom and clarify your paths."

Km 10, Crta. Tulum-Boca Paila; 877/265-4139; betulum.com. **$$$**

Be Tulum's restaurant and pool area.

A lounge in Coqui Coqui Tulum Residence & Spa's main house.

A peek into one of the guest rooms at Ahau Tulum.

2 Coqui Coqui Tulum Residence & Spa

In the center of Tulum's "Zona Yoga," this rough-hewn beach house was transformed into an intimate inn by husband-and-wife owners Francesca Bonato, an Italian designer, and Nicolas Malleville, an Argentine model. The couple draw an international network of beautiful people (Jade Jagger and Sienna Miller are regulars). Seven cool, dimly lit concrete guest rooms exude a vampire glamour, as does the mostly black lobby, which doubles as a highbrow gift shop of sorts. Stock up on leather jewelry, silk rebozo shawls, and unisex scents made with agave, mint, and lime.

Km 7.5, Crta. Tulum-Boca Paila; 52-984/100-1400; coquicoquispa.com. **$$**

3 Ahau Tulum

Club impresario David Graziano left the fast-paced New York City nightlife scene behind for his latest project, a village of thatched-roof beach cabanas along the sun-drenched Caribbean shore. The property's eco-friendly angle is evident at every turn: a sustainable garden is fed by a rainwater-catchment system, and the restaurant is powered by solar panels and wind turbines. The 20 rooms adhere to a simple, natural aesthetic with their woven A-frame ceilings, native hardwood floors, handcrafted furnishings, and patios shaded by palm fronds. Walls of windows keep the focus where it should be—on the waves beyond.

Km 7, Crta. Tulum-Boca Paila; 52-984/167-1154; ahautulum.com. **$$**

mexico+central+south america

81

The veranda at
Belcampo Lodge's
main pavilion,
Machaca Hill.

Fresh salsas made with produce from Belcampo's farm. Right: The resort's pool area.

PUNTA GORDA, BELIZE

Belcampo Lodge

Farm-to-table, meet jungle to-table. Deep within the rain forest between the Maya Mountains and the Caribbean Sea, the 12-suite Belcampo Lodge is more field expedition than farm stay—albeit with modern perks like Wi-Fi and AC. Private cottages nail the indoor-outdoor aesthetic, thanks to screened porches with hammocks overlooking canopies of gumbo-limbo trees. Guests can tour the 1,000-acre working farm and cocoa nursery, embark on guided foraging trips for exotic edibles like cassava and *culantro,* or spy howler monkeys on an adjacent 12,000-acre wilderness reserve. The estate is the source of nearly everything on the menu at the lodge's restaurant, from the poached eggs served on boiled *chaya* leaves at breakfast to the mint muddled in the mojito during cocktail hour.

Wilson Rd.; 888/299-9940; belcampoinc.com. **$$$**

The pool deck at Trump Ocean Club, with the Bay of Panama beyond.

Trump Ocean Club

If the current wave of five-star hotels is any indication, Panama City—a onetime haven for shady characters and shadier dealings—is clearly on the upswing. At the forefront of this real-estate boom: the sail-like, 369-room Trump Ocean Club, in the tony Punta Pacifica neighborhood. Everything here is appropriately over-the-top, from the slick amenities (custom mini-bars; personalized stationery) and modern flourishes (banana boat-shaped freestanding tubs) to the private-island beach accessible by catamaran. Links lovers head straight for the 18-hole golf course, then share scores over icy Seco Herrerano cocktails at the nearby yacht club. Most guests choose to while away the day on the 13th-floor terrace, where cabanas surround five pools with views of the water. But don't miss the fresh Latin-Caribbean seafood at Tejas; it goes from fishing boat to plate in a matter of hours.

Calle Punta Colón; 855/255-9640 or 011-507/215-8800; trumphotelcollection.com. **$$$**

PANAMA CITY

Las Clementinas

Writer Graham Greene would have felt right at home at Las Clementinas, in Panama City's atmospheric Casco Viejo (Old Town). A maze of stairs in the restored 1930's apartment building leads you to one of six suites, each equipped with a full kitchen and outfitted in custom details: floors crafted from guayacan wood reclaimed from the bottom of the Canal; beds made of longleaf pine sourced from defunct U.S. Army barracks; and desks recovered from the old British Embassy. Explore the neighborhood's 17th-century cathedral and crumbling mansions, then retreat to the hotel's Secret Garden, which is set against a colonial fort wall standing 30 feet below street level. Diplomats and backpackers alike go for the spicy *guacho de mariscos*, a traditional Caribbean stew, and martinis infused with fresh-picked basil.

Corner of Avda. B and Calle 11 Este; 877/889-0351 or 011-507/228-7613; lasclementinas.com. $$

One of the hotel's high-ceilinged suites.

Costa Rica

Deserted stretches of sand. Endlessly diverse wildlife refuges. A laid-back *pura vida* lifestyle. What's not to love about Costa Rica? Sure, it's been on the adventure lover's radar for a while, but with a host of small, exquisitely designed hotels hidden in the jungle and along the shore, the tiny Central American country is now more appealing than ever. Here, three places to drop the backpack.

NICARAGUA

ARENAL VOLCANO NATIONAL PARK

2

NICOYA PENINSULA

3

SAN JOSÉ

1

PACIFIC OCEAN

1 Oxygen Jungle Villas

A steep gravel road brings you to this remote retreat above the town of Uvita. The first thing you see is the pool, edged with Moroccan lanterns and chaises where guests lie under Balinese umbrellas. The 12 teak-roofed glass bungalows are furnished with four-poster beds, stacks of baskets that serve as dressers, and large white sofas. If there's something disconcerting about staying in such upscale digs in the middle of the jungle, rest assured: you'll quickly adjust.

Uvita; 506/8322-4773; oxygenjunglevillas.com. $

Balinese umbrellas and lounge chairs at Oxygen Jungle Villas.

An authentic meal at El Silencio Lodge & Spa's restaurant.

Cala Luna's pool and adjacent bar area, under a shady *palapa*.

2 Cala Luna

For those who'd prefer to dip in and out of the lively scene in surfer-friendly Tamarindo, there's Cala Luna, less than two miles south on the almost empty Playa Langosta. Rooms and villas are as sensitive to the environment as they are easy on the eyes, using only natural and recycled materials and done up in cool beiges; polished concrete walls, locally made furniture, and mosaic-tiled bathtubs add to the visual interest. There's horseback riding at the owners' ranch, a few minutes away, and whale-watching aboard the hotel's 26-foot powerboat. Just get back in time for sunset at Cala Luna's intimate beach.

Playa Langosta; 855/522-5258 or 506/2653-0214; calaluna.com. **$$**

3 El Silencio Lodge & Spa

Tangaras, quetzals, smiling sloths—you'll find them all at this 500-acre hideaway in a tropical cloud forest. The property resembles a Japanese mountain village: 16 wooden bungalows built on pillars rise above exotic ferns and gargantuan leaves. The rustic-chic interiors are the work of Costa Rican architect Ronald Zurcher, who incorporated lacquered-wood floors, bamboo ceilings, and decks overlooking mist-ringed mountains. At night, head to the glass-walled Las Ventanas restaurant to feast on such Central American specialties as spicy chicken chalupas made with ingredients sourced from El Silencio's organic farm.

Bajos de Toro Amarillo Sarchi; 506/2231-6122; silenciolodge.com. **$$**

Early-20th-
century details in
a guest room at
Casa Gangotena.

QUITO, ECUADOR

Casa Gangotena

South American trendsetters have christened Quito the continent's next great getaway. Just in time for this style-centric wave of travelers comes Casa Gangotena, a 1926 mansion that recently emerged from a three-year, $11 million renovation. Located on Plaza San Francisco in the historic San Roque neighborhood, the property has 31 guest rooms whose 12-foot ceilings are embellished with Art Nouveau molded tiles and restored plasterwork friezes. Beds are topped with plush goose-feather duvets, while white-and-gray Statuarietto marble bathrooms are filled with sunlight from luminescent stained-glass windows. Book a second-floor suite for views of Pichincha Volcano looming in the distance, or kick back on the rooftop terrace for a 360-degree panorama of the towers and spires of this UNESCO-listed city. Later, head downstairs, where chef Andrés Dávila reimagines Ecuadoran specialties using green plantains and Andean potatoes purchased daily at the nearby farmers' market.

6-41 Bolívar Oeste y Cuenca; 593-2/400-8000; casagangotena.com. **$$$**

A view toward the Plaza San Francisco and the surrounding hills of Quito.

Mashpi Lodge

A bedroom
nestled in the
rain forest at
Mashpi Lodge.

Like a sophisticated version of Tarzan's lair, Mashpi Lodge is a glass-enclosed eco-haven set four miles into Ecuador's 3,200-acre Mashpi Rainforest Biodiversity Reserve. Here, you can hitch a gondola ride through the cloud forest canopy, swim in the secluded Cucharillos and San Vicente waterfalls, and discover innumerable species of animal life with a resident biologist. No reason to rely on your newfound foraging skills for lunch, what with expertly made shrimp ceviche on the menu. After a long day in the wild, retire to one of the property's 22 rooms, where rich sapele-wood accents offset crisp white cotton linens (and an overnight laundry service takes care of muddy clothes). All this, just three hours from Quito's frenetic hum, but worlds away in spirit.

Sector La Delicia; 888/527-0166; mashpilodge.com; all-inclusive; two-night minimum. **$$$$$**

Palacio Nazarenas

A guest suite
at Palacio
Nazarenas.

The history of this mansion and 16th-century convent on the Plaza de Armas is nothing if not dramatic (think clashing conquistadors and nuns wearing crowns of thorns). The present, however, is decidedly less conflicted: with the help of a team of architects and archaeologists, Orient-Express has rehabilitated the building into a 55-suite hotel in the heart of the budding San Blas neighborhood. Pre-Columbian artifacts salvaged during the four-year excavation are on display in the original structure, now also home to a spa with glass-floored treatment rooms that peer down on unearthed Inca walls and an ancient canal. A two-story annex provides a contemporary twist in the form of Cuzco's first outdoor infinity pool and an upscale Peruvian restaurant helmed by native superstar chef Virgilio Martínez. As at any modern hotel in town, oxygen is pumped into guest rooms to alleviate altitude sickness—so rest easy; in the morning, Machu Picchu awaits.

144 Plaza Nazarenas; 51-1/610-8300; palacionazarenas.com. **$$$$**

The outdoor infinity pool, adjacent to the hotel's original structure.

PATAGONIA, CHILE

Tierra Patagonia Hotel & Spa

On the edge of the 600,000-acre Torres del Paine National Park, this low-slung lakefront escape emerges from a windswept hillside along the Patagonian pampas. It's the second hotel from the Tierra Hotels group: the first, Tierra Atacama, lured adventure seekers to the far reaches of Chile's northern desert. Here in the south, the elegantly understated rooms come with widescreen views of Lago Sarmiento and are stocked with artisan-crafted local comforts (handwoven throw blankets; armchairs upholstered in light Patagonian wool). Three duplex loft suites capitalize on additional space, but the best moments at the hotel occur beyond your *lenga*-wood-paneled guest quarters— around the tiled infinity pool, in the 3,500-square-foot Uma spa, or on one of the nearly 50 bespoke excursions. In these surroundings, even a simple afternoon spent sheepshearing with gauchos becomes an otherworldly experience.

Ruta 9 and Ruta Y156, Torres del Paine; 56-2/370-5301; tierrapatagonia.com; all-inclusive; three-night minimum. **$$$$$**

Looking out on mountain-fringed Lago Sarmiento at Tierra Patagonia Hotel & Spa.

A guest room at Singular Patagonia, backed by Last Hope Sound.

Singular Patagonia

Here's a challenge: take a century-old meat-storage facility on the shoals of Patagonia's icy fjords and turn it into a top-notch adventure resort. The Santiago-based Singular brand has proved more than up to the task. For the group's first hotel venture, designer Enrique Concha helped transform the brick-and-timber structure (located an hour from Torres del Paine National Park) into a cavernous main lodge with dramatic walls of glass. Fifty-seven guest rooms look onto Last Hope Sound and the snowcapped Andes. After breakfast, set forth on staff-arranged excursions that include kayaking along the Río Golondrina and treks through two for-guests-only reserves, just a short motorboat ride away.

56-61/722-030; thesingular.com; all-inclusive. **$$$$**

Hotel Fasano Boa Vista

Can Fasano get any hotter? The sexy São Paulo hotel group recently added a fourth property to its portfolio—this one an understated retreat on a 2,800-acre farm an hour's drive northwest of the company's home base. Brazilian architect Isay Weinfeld (who also designed Fasano's first retreat in Punta del Este, Uruguay) used golden-brown freijo wood for the living-room-style lobby, with its triple-height windows and mid-20th-century furnishings. The 39 light-filled guest rooms echo the earthy vibe with glowing hardwood floors and mosaic-tiled limestone walls. Large verandas in the suites face undulating green hills; fireplaces and rocking chairs beckon upon arrival (go ahead, the staff will unpack for you). Meanwhile, the restaurant honors Fasano's Italian-Brazilian culinary tradition with smoked-ricotta cappelletti in an *amatriciana* sauce. A spa, an infinity-edged pool, and a private lake for swimming are just a quick stroll across the grass—you'll want to go barefoot, of course.

Km 102.5, Rodovia Castello Branco; 55-15/3261-9900; fasano.com.br. **$$$$**

A terrace on Hotel Fasano Boa Vista's private lake.

A shaded corner on Pousada do Toque's pool deck.

SÃO MIGUEL DOS MILAGRES, BRAZIL

Pousada do Toque

Crashing waves and crooning curassows—that's all you'll hear at the Pousada do Toque, a stylish seaside retreat enshrouded by a bird-filled jungle garden in the Alagoas region of northeastern Brazil. The inn is rustic but not rugged: warm-hued furnishings throughout the grounds were crafted from native hardwoods (in the lounge, imbuia chairs by designer Sergio Rodrigues are more comfortable than they look), and luxuries like air-conditioning, flat-screen televisions, and Trussardi linens make the 17 cabana-style guest rooms feel modern. Meals in the airy dining room are outstanding, a testament to owner Nilo Burgarelli's experience as a restaurateur; don't miss the *peixe ao molho de camarão,* made with locally caught fish and herbs grown on site and topped with a hearty shrimp-and-tomato sauce. After lunch, venture half a mile offshore to explore the resident coral reef, where foot-deep tide pools are filled with aquamarine water and tiny scuttling crabs.

Rua Felisberto do Ataide; 55-82/3295-1127; pousadadotoque.com.br. **$$$**

A seating area in the hotel's lounge. Above: Wooden details in a guest room.

Hotel Unique's curving, window-studded exterior.

Hotel Unique

Design junkies will find plenty to love at Hotel Unique, the eight-story, watermelon-slice-shaped brainchild of Brazilian architect Ruy Ohtake. As might be expected from a former apprentice to Oscar Niemeyer, geometry is the star here, seen in curved hallways, sloped walls, and oversize circular windows that resemble portholes. Frosted glass surfaces with inset flat-screen televisions divide sleep and lounge areas in some of the 95 Modernist guest rooms; suites have wooden floors that arch all the way up to the ceiling. In keeping with the theme, there's also a rounded library stocked with 300 books on design, architecture, and fashion. The final touch to Hotel Unique's eye-pleasing panoply? The stunning views of Ibirapuera Park and the São Paulo skyline, best appreciated from the crimson-tiled rooftop pool.

4700 Ave. Brigadeiro Luís Antônio; 55-11/3055-4710; hotelunique.com.br. **$$$$**

mexico+central+south america

103

A sitting area in Aguas Arriba Lodge, overlooking Lago del Desierto.

Aguas Arriba Lodge

Until recently, large swaths of Argentinean Patagonia were almost impenetrable. But now that the seven-room Aguas Arriba has opened on a steep, forested shore above the trout-filled Lago del Desierto, travelers finally have a place to rest their heads. Getting there is an adventure in itself: the one-hour drive to the lake's edge from the trekking village of El Chaltén traverses a seriously rutted gravel road. You can then take a scenic 15-minute boat ride to the property—or embark on a three-hour hike through the heart of the forest. The lodge is elegant yet simple; there's no concierge, per se, and each staffer serves triple duty. Your host/masseuse/yoga teacher may lead you on a walk past *lenga* trees and wild orchids before depositing you on your lakefront porch for a dinner of beef fillet and baked pears in Burgundy sauce. Heeding the call of the wild, after all, needn't mean depriving yourself of creature comforts.

Km 130, Ruta Provincial Norte 23; 54-11/4152-5697; aguasarribalodge.com; all-inclusive. **$$$$**

Mio

Argentina's latest oenophile retreat can be found not in the vineyards of Salta but on the streets of Recoleta, B.A.'s poshest neighborhood. Mio's entrance is certainly impressive, marked by two 20-foot-tall doors fashioned out of Malbec-stained barrel slats from the Mendoza estate of its owner, the wife of celebrated vintner César Catena. In the 30 guest rooms, wine-colored recliners evoke the spoils of just-harvested grapes, and a custom dispenser in your bedroom pours Prosecco whenever you want it. Artistic standouts vie for attention, be it a sensuous tub carved from native *caldén* wood or the tiered waterfall adorned with bold metal butterflies. In the black-stone spa, alternate between dips in the solar-heated pool and deep-tissue treatments using (what else?) a soothing Tempranillo.

465 Avda. Presidente Manuel Quintana; 54-11/5295-8500; miobuenosaires.com. **$$$**

Minimalist touches in a bedroom at Mio.

105

A porter in the
trompe l'oeil lobby
of La Maison
Champs-Élysées,
in Paris.

Europe

The Pig's
conservatory
dining room.

BROCKENHURST, ENGLAND

The Pig

When it comes to the new breed of English country house hotels, Hampshire's Lime Wood has been the retreat to beat. Now the property's little sister—a diminutive charmer just 15 minutes away—is stealing the spotlight. At the Pig, an inviting Anglo-chic sensibility has transformed what was once a dark manor house into a stylish inn. Sitting areas are appointed with wing chairs and working fireplaces, while the 26 guest rooms have claw-foot bathtubs and botanical prints. In the dining room, chef James Golding (a protégé of celebrated British restaurateur Mark Hix) cooks seasonal, locally sourced food in simple, unpretentious combinations, serving house-cured salmon as well as all manner of piggy parts, roasted, smoked, or salted. Just outside the door: the staggeringly green New Forest National Park, where Golding and his staff foraged many of the ingredients on your plate.

Beaulieu Rd.; 44-1590/622-354; thepighotel.com. **$$**

The inn's ivy-covered exterior. Above: A cozy reading nook.

europe

109

LONDON

Bulgari Hotel & Residences

A living room
in Suite I at
Bulgari Hotel &
Residences.

The latest addition to Bulgari's hotel empire is a glamorous haunt for those who aren't afraid of the dark—think gleaming mahogany, polished black granite, and precious metals. Rising just opposite Hyde Park, the property is the work of Milan-based architects and designers Antonio Citterio and Patricia Viel, who referenced the Italian fashion house's lavish jewelry collections with metallized fabric in the restaurant and covered the ceiling in Il Bar with sheets of hammered titanium. The opulence continues in the 85 guest rooms (the largest in London), which have onyx baths, silvery brocade headboards, and vintage Moroccan carpets; at turndown, your butler lights scented votives tub-side. If that isn't enough to help you channel your inner Roman emperor, a copy of Marcus Aurelius's *Meditations* awaits on the nightstand.

171 Knightsbridge; 44-20/7151-1010; bulgarihotels.com. **$$$$**

One of the four
guest rooms at
the Orange Public
House & Hotel.

Pan-fried cod with roasted carrots. Left: The main dining room.

Orange Public House & Hotel

Pretty young things from nearby Chelsea and Belgravia pack the Orange Public House every evening. But look closely: this modern British gastropub has a secret. Tucked in the back is a narrow set of stairs that leads to four rustic-luxe bedrooms—each small yet cozy, with bleached wood paneling, slate-tiled bathrooms, Egyptian-cotton linens, and a vintage radio. Dormer windows overlook the Regency-era town houses, antiques dealers, and homegrown boutiques of the fashionable Pimlico neighborhood. (David Linley has a furniture atelier steps away; milliner Philip Treacy's showroom is on Elizabeth Street.) Stick around for the pub's classic Sunday roast, made with dry-aged beef and served with Yorkshire pudding, or make like the locals and wander down the road to Daylesford Organic for a farm-to-table take on afternoon tea.

37 Pimlico Rd.; 44-20/7730-0070; theorange.co.uk. **$$**

europe

113

InterContinental Palacio das Cardosas

A 200-year-old Neoclassical façade is all that remains of the original Palacio das Cardosas, a palace turned monastery on Porto's main square that is now the site of InterContinental's first Portuguese property. Crystal chandeliers, intricate ceiling moldings, and inlaid-marble flooring hint at the building's former life, but the 105 bright guest rooms are firmly rooted in the present with spacious rain showers and mirrored tiles behind the beds. Order a port tasting at the wood-paneled Bar de Cardosas, then have the staff arrange for a tour of nearby Vila Nova de Gaia to get a firsthand account of how the wine is aged. For local specialties like slow-roasted *leitão* (suckling pig), grab a window seat at the hotel's Astória restaurant, the best place in town to admire the Praça da Liberdade's Belle Époque grandeur.

25 Praça da Liberdade; 800/327-0200 or 351/220-035-600; ichotelsgroup.com. $$

A street view of the InterContinental Palacio das Cardosas, on the Praça da Liberdade.

Jumeirah Port Sóller Hotel & Spa

The only potential downside of a stay at the Jumeirah Port Sóller: the visual fatigue that results from the sheer volume of jaw-dropping views. There's the Mediterranean on one side, the Tramuntana Mountains on the other, and fragrant citrus groves everywhere in between (hence the freshly squeezed orange juice at check-in). Set on a rocky promontory on the northwestern coast, the 120 rooms keep the focus on the landscape with muted beige interiors and walls of windows. You can take in the vistas from the cliff-hugging infinity pool or during an ayurvedic body treatment at the light-filled spa. Then watch the sun set from the top-floor lounge, where golden bulbs twinkle against the darkening sky.

Calle Bélgica; 34/97-163-7888; jumeirah.com. **$$$**

A heated swimming pool at Jumeirah Port Sóller Hotel & Spa.

An understated
guest room at
Primero Primera.

Primero Primera

You can count the Catalan bourgeoisie among your neighbors at the family-owned Primero Primera hotel, a converted 1950's building in the residential enclave of Tres Torres. Despite such modern touches as hanging metal lamps and slate-hued walls, an old-world spirit prevails, thanks to antique furnishings and sepia-toned photographs of the owners' ancestors. The 30 rooms are small yet comfortable, with goose-down duvets and warm wooden vanities; many overlook the neighborhood's tree-lined lanes and small row houses. Mornings start with *café con leche* on a walled-in patio dotted with wrought-iron tables. Quiet evenings are spent curled up in one of the plush leather armchairs in the club-style lobby lounge. When you yearn to take part in Barcelona's urban bustle, Las Ramblas and the cobblestoned streets of the Barri Gòtic are 10 minutes away.

25-29 Doctor Carulla; 34/93-417-5600; primeroprimera.com. **$$**

The villa's landscaped garden. Below: A black-and-white guest room.

ÎLE DE RÉ, FRANCE

Villa Clarisse

It can't be long before the crowds descend on picturesque Île de Ré. This under-the-radar summer getaway off France's Atlantic Coast is just too beautiful to remain undiscovered. The same can be said for the petite Villa Clarisse, which has remained a virtual secret until now. Sister property to the polished Hôtel de Toiras in the port of St. Martin de Ré, this 18th-century inn is unfussy and fashionably rustic, tucked in a residential neighborhood a three-minute walk from the harbor. The nine guest rooms, designed by Pierre-Yves Rochon and owner Olivia Le Calvez, have antique desks, whitewashed walls, and green shutters that open to garden views. Only breakfast and lunch are served on site, which means you're free to make the short stroll to town for a glass of the local rosé and succulent oysters right off the boat.

5 Rue du Général Lapasset; 33-5/46-68-43-00; villa-clarisse.fr. **$$**

La Maison Champs-Élysées

The White Lounge at La Maison Champs-Élysées.

Once the residence of the Duchess of Rivoli, this 19th-century edifice in the heart of the city's Golden Triangle blends seamlessly with the iconic Haussmann façades that surround it. Yet thanks to French fashion house Maison Martin Margiela, what lies inside is equal parts playful and provocative. La Maison Champs-Élysées is not your standard Parisian pied-à-terre: in the lobby, mirrors reflect the stark White Lounge and a *gothique* cigar bar with dark-as-night walls. One-off details like slipcovered sofas and honeycomb-shaped chairs mix with unfinished moldings and trompe l'oeil wallpaper in some of the 57 rooms. Yes, more traditional comforts remain—including linens from Garnier Thiebaut and goose-down duvets—but the hotel's balance of elegance and eccentricity turns conventional luxury into something far more chic.

8 Rue Jean Goujon, Eighth Arr.; 33-1/40-74-64-65; lamaisonchampselysees.com. **$$$**

The hotel's black Curiosity Case Suite.

One of Le Bristol's St.-Honoré suites.

Le Bristol

One-upmanship has been the name of the game among the city's vaunted palace hotels, and this grande dame—emerging from a $130 million renovation—is no exception. Thankfully, the tasteful redesign kept all of the good things (19th-century paintings; gilded ceilings) while infusing the space with a lighter, more welcoming sensibility. Floor-to-ceiling windows lend an airy feel to the new La Prairie spa, and the Michelin three-starred Epicure restaurant has been completely redone, with romantic tables for two overlooking the leafy courtyard. An original wrought-iron elevator brings you upstairs to two novel St.-Honoré suites with Louis XVI–style furnishings. And in the cream-colored Matignon wing, a staircase is now brightened by a winding, seven-story illuminated installation— an addition perfectly suited for the City of Light.

112 Rue du Faubourg St.-Honoré; 800/745-8883 or 33-1/53-43-43-00; lebristolparis.com. **$$$$**

europe

Paris

The ideal Parisian hotel is like a *macaron*—small, colorful, and bursting with flavor. But in reality, too many boutique properties miss the mark. How to tell the winners from the duds? Follow our guide to the city's most intimate bolt-holes, which encompass styles both traditional (a nostalgic town house near the Luxembourg Gardens) and contemporary (an art-filled hangout by the Louvre). The sweetest part: all have rates starting at less than $250 a night.

1 Hôtel Amour

At this 24-room favorite, restaurant royalty Thierry Costes and artist and nightlife celeb Mr. André splurged on high-thread-count sheets, Kiehl's products, and striking design details (jewel-toned lacquer walls; original photography; collectible toys) while spurning needless amenities for the laptop generation, such as TV's and phones. A lively bistro—serving one of the most hopping brunches in Paris—draws many of the cool kids enlivening the Ninth.

8 Rue Navarin, Ninth Arr.; 33-1/48-78-31-80; hotelamourparis.fr. **$**

A diner at Hôtel Amour's Bistro restaurant.

Le Crayon's Delightful Drawings room.

One of two "Sous les Toits" rooms at Hôtel Jules & Jim.

▣ Le Crayon

Four blocks north of the Louvre, Le Crayon is all about a "handmade" hotel experience; it's as though guests were staying in the residence of a local artist—namely that of its decorator, Julie Gauthron. A poetic, patchwork approach to prints and styles results in a good-humored mash-up: the 26 rooms feature boldly patterned wallpapers, offbeat geometric mirrors, Panton chairs, and spruced-up flea-market finds such as articulated lamps and marble-topped nightstands. Breakfast is served in a basement-level dining room outfitted with funky vintage furniture, though you can also savor your croissants in bed.

25 Rue du Bouloi, First Arr.; 33-1/42-36-54-19; hotelcrayon.com. **$**

▣ Hôtel Jules & Jim

A discreet gray façade marks this gem in the Upper Marais. Its concept: art gallery meets lounge meets hotel, where you'll bump into locals as often as out-of-towners. Three buildings, including an 18th-century house, are clustered around a cobblestoned courtyard outfitted with a vertical garden, a fireplace, and a café that peddles breakfast by day and cocktails at night. A palette of inviting neutrals (ecru, café au lait, chocolate) and arty photos documenting the hotel's renovation define the 23 rooms. For a view of the Sacré Coeur, ask for a street-facing room on the seventh or eighth floor.

11 Rue des Gravilliers, Third Arr.; 33-1/44-54-13-13; hoteljulesetjim.com. **$$**

The street outside Hôtel Saint-Louis en L'Isle.

4 Hôtel Saint-Louis en L'Isle

The Île St.-Louis is picture-book Paris, its narrow streets lined with cafés, *boulangeries,* and, of course, the original Berthillon ice cream shop. This hotel, 20 rooms in a renovated 19th-century building, sustains that sense of well-polished nostalgia. A twist of your fleur-de-lis-shaped room key reveals stone floors and tufted velvet headboards. Other thoughtful details—such as the loaner iPads loaded with weather, currency, and translation apps— belie the reasonable price. So does the central location: the Latin Quarter, the Marais, and Notre Dame are all just a bridge span away.

75 Rue St.-Louis en l'Île, Fourth Arr.; 33-1/46-34-04-80; saintlouisenlisle.com. **$$**

Vintage details at Hôtel de la Paix.

Hôtel de la Porte Dorée's lobby sitting area.

5 Hôtel de la Paix

Behind a sober Art Deco–era exterior is a sitting room sprinkled with artifacts culled from the owners' travels and family archives: old books; Chinese statues; a phonograph. Bustling street notwithstanding, the 39 diminutive rooms have a vintage country appeal, with shutters repurposed as headboards and *boutis* bedspreads topped with multihued pillows. The location—which straddles the border of the Sixth and 14th— is ideal for would-be regulars at such iconic restaurants as Le Dôme, Le Select, and La Coupole; one block south is the Fondation Cartier contemporary art center, known for its cutting-edge exhibits.

225 Blvd. Raspail, 14th Arr.; 33-1/43-20-35-82; paris-montparnasse-hotel.com. **$**

6 Hôtel de la Porte Dorée

Located on the city's residential eastern fringe, a couple of avenues from the Bois de Vincennes, this stately building feels like a bourgeois town house, with 43 rooms on four floors and a towering bookshelf on every landing. Lovingly renovated by Franco-American owners, who stocked the place with antiques, the hotel recently received a Green Key award for adopting energy efficient operations and serving free-trade coffee at breakfast. Traveling with kids? You're a five-minute walk from the tropical aquarium at the Palais de la Porte Dorée and the boats and pony rides at Lac Daumesnil.

273 Ave. Daumesnil, 12th Arr.; 33-1/43-07-56-97; hoteldelaportedoree.com. **$**

Au Vieux Panier

At the vanguard of the hotel-as-gallery trend, Au Vieux Panier isn't just a place to spend the night: it's an immersive art installation, reconceived annually by a rotating cast and set within a 17th-century former grocery store in Marseilles' oldest district. Each of the six guest rooms is the singular expression of its designer's style. In one, the night sky appears to shimmer overhead thanks to phosphorescent microorganisms; in another, psychedelic and baroque influences battle for dominance, with every inch layered in kaleidoscopic Escher and Art Deco patterns. But this year's standout has to be the bipolar Panic Room by French tagger Tilt, who slathered half the space in dense, neon graffiti, leaving the rest stark white—the visual equivalent of switching radio stations from floor-shaking hip-hop to ambient trance. Which side of the bed would you choose?

13 Rue du Panier; 33-4/91-91-23-72; auvieuxpanier.com. $

The Panic Room suite at Au Vieux Panier.

Colorful rafts
hanging above
Mama Shelter
Marseilles' bar.

A bright guest-room alcove. Right: The hotel's low-lit bar.

MARSEILLES, FRANCE

Mama Shelter

Opened four years after its Parisian parent, this slightly smaller baby-Shelter—in Marseilles' up-and-coming Cours Julien neighborhood—gives urban minimalism a street-smart spin. The hotel comes courtesy of Philippe Starck, who expanded on his whimsical bric-a-brac aesthetic by infusing public spaces with the warm tones and aquatic touches of the Midi region. Aluminum octopi drip over the hotel's entranceway; ceilings are lined with graffitied chalkboards; rainbow-bright inflatable rafts hang above the bar. A pink foosball table channels the spirit of a traditional *pétanque* court. By contrast, each of the 123 rooms is a little Zen koan for the 21st century: bare cement walls, pastel accents, and embedded Apple TV's. At all hours, guests crowd into the Alain Senderens restaurant for chorizo-and-cherry-tomato pizza—so good it's almost enough to make you forget about the hotel's beach 15 minutes away.

64 Rue de la Loubière; 33-4/84-35-20-00; mamashelter.com. **$**

europe

La Maison d'Olivier Leflaive

When guests of the Burgundy vintner Olivier Leflaive begged for a place to sleep off the celebrated 14-wine tastings at his Puligny-Montrachet winery, he created a cozy inn nearby in a restored 17th-century manse. Exposed beams and embroidered bedcovers distinguish the 13 rooms, whose rust-colored shutters open onto a well-tended garden. Of course, the focus at the restaurant is on the area's biodynamic whites and reds; prix fixe menus pair Meursaults, Volnays, and Pommards with hearty terrines and chicken fricassees. Sommeliers lead the tastings, along with workshops held daily in the vineyard and visits to the cellar, where the family—established in the region since 1717—ages some 800,000 bottles a year.

10 Place du Monument, Puligny-Montrachet; 33-3/80-21-95-27; maison-olivierleflaive.fr. **$**

The Soleil Atmosphere room at La Maison d'Olivier Leflaive.

La Plage Casadelmar's low-key pool area.

La Plage Casadelmar

French architect Jean-François Bodin has brought his trademark restraint to Porto-Vecchio, the St.-Tropez of Corsica. At La Plage Casadelmar, the famed minimalist created 15 rooms out of volcanic rock and 300-year-old oaks. Sergio Rodrigues chairs and Ozone lamps speak to the pared-down sensibility, but all points lead outward—the horizontal lines of the reception desk draw the eye to infinite vistas; the crushed-marble floor, like a sandy path, carries feet to the beach. The restaurant serves comforting Mediterranean fare (grilled fish; Tropézienne brioches with whipped cream). The overall effect is that of a family house filled with memories that every year brings you back to the sea.

Presqu'île du Benedettu; 33-4/95-71-02-30; laplagecasadelmar.fr. **$$$$**

A view from Hotel Castello di Casole's Tosca restaurant. Above: The estate's rolling hills.

SIENA, ITALY

Hotel Castello di Casole

Blue blood is no longer a prerequisite for a stay in the hilltop Castello di Casole, a refurbished 10th-century castle at the center of a 4,200-acre Tuscan estate. That doesn't mean you won't feel like an aristocrat. A cypress-lined road takes you through vineyard-dotted landscapes and past a collection of revamped 18th-century stone farmhouses—all available for weekly rentals—to 41 suites that mix old-school details (oil paintings; reclaimed terra-cotta) with such modern luxuries as radiant floor heating. When not taking lessons from an expert local ceramicist or enjoying a concert at the on-site amphitheater, guests can set off on wild-boar hunts near the castle's grounds, as its erstwhile residents did. Back at the hotel's stone-walled Tosca restaurant, Daniele Sera turns out masterful updates of Italian classics like risotto with braised veal shank—when he's not serving as a private chef for the Moroccan royal family.

53031 Casole d'Elsa, Località Querceto; 39-0577/961-508; castellodicasole.com. **$$$$**

A spacious
suite in the
hotel's
main villa.

CIVITA DI BAGNOREGIO, ITALY

Corte della Maestà

It takes some effort to reach the remote outpost of Civita di Bagnoregio, which teeters on a bluff 80 miles from Rome: the only way in is a steep uphill walk via a quarter-mile-long footbridge. Pass through Civita's main gate, first carved out of the mountain by Etruscans 2,500 years ago, and you'll find a crumbling time capsule of ivy-clad arches; crooked, cobblestoned lanes; and sun-flooded piazzas. It's here that Italian novelist and TV personality Paolo Crepet opened Corte della Maestà, inside a bishop's residence from the sixth century. The stone-walled retreat has five cozy rooms with names like the Abbess and the Writer, embellished with antique furniture and art (a 16th-century fresco here, an Art Nouveau cast-iron stove there). Spend an afternoon picking figs, apples, and other treats from the inn's garden, then unwind at the Turkish steam bath— your exertions to get here a distant memory.

Vicolo della Maestà; 39-0761/792-548; cortedellamaesta.com. **$$$**

The hilltop village of Civita di Bagnoregio.

Rome

Romans are staunchly loyal to their own *rioni*, or districts; it follows that the best way to get an insider experience of the city's most desirable quarters is to check in to one of the small neighborhood inns that manifest the energy and aesthetic of the surrounding streets. Here, three places that fill the bill perfectly, providing a warm welcome and a caliber of service that would earn praise regardless of your allegiances.

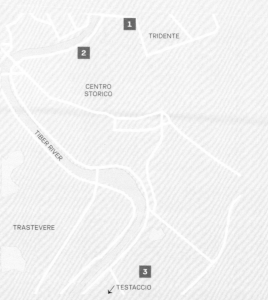

1 TRIDENTE

2

CENTRO STORICO

TIBER RIVER

TRASTEVERE

3

TESTACCIO

1 Residenza Napoleone III

In the bustling Tridente area, the two-apartment Residenza Napoleone has been restored to its 1830's splendor. Antiques and hand-stenciled walls complement 16th-century tapestries in the three-room Napoleone Suite; the more modern Roof Garden Suite has a terrace that offers views of the Spanish Steps. The building is still occupied by Princess Letizia Ruspoli, who is effectively your innkeeper, though it is her second-in-command who sees to the details of your stay.

56 Via della Fontanella di Borghese; 39-347/733-7098; residenzanapoleone.com.
$$$$

The Napoleone Suite at Residenza Napoleone III.

Gigli d'Oro Suite's amiable doorman.

The covered patio at Hotel San Anselmo.

2 Gigli d'Oro Suite

For an ideal base in Rome's *centro storico*, look no further than the Gigli d'Oro Suite, housed in a discreet renovated palace dating back to the 15th century. Each of the six guest rooms harbors at least one original architectural detail, whether it be the massive beams in the Stelletta Suite or the granite fireplace in the rooftop Maschera d'Oro Suite. A bright, compact breakfast lounge is transformed into a (complimentary) cocktail bar in the evening. And the hotel's ultra-solicitous staff can dispense advice on everything from purchasing exhibition tickets to finding the best *polpette*.

12 Via dei Gigli d'Oro; 39-06/6839-2055; giglidorosuite.com. **$$$**

3 Hotel San Anselmo

Located at the edge of the vibrant Testaccio neighborhood, the 34-room Hotel San Anselmo is a genteel and gracious retreat. The hotel's garden is lush with orange trees and outfitted with green iron tables; equally tranquil is the lounge, with its long glass wall facing the garden. Room 829 has limed parquet floors and a romantically curtained bed, but the rest skew flamboyant with dramatic chandeliers and frescoes. Guests seek out many of the area's authentic pleasures: a perfect *ristretto* at Pasticceria Linari, or a walk through Volpetti, where jams made by Trappist nuns are arranged like jewels.

2 Piazza di Sant'Anselmo; 39-06/570-057; aventinohotels.com. **$$**

House-made nut cookies at I Casali del Pino. Left: The farm's kitchen.

I Casali del Pino

Ilaria Venturini Fendi may be a scion of the Roman fashion dynasty—but this accessory designer's primary passion is her organic farm and *agriturismo,* 30 minutes outside Rome. There's nothing overtly glamorous about I Casali del Pino's 19 rustic-chic rooms, which come with salvaged tiles, wrought-iron beds, and under-floor geothermal heating. Guests can look on as farmhands create organic pecorino in the on-site cheese-making facility, stroll among the resident donkeys and chickens, or shop for totes crafted from "upcycled" materials (Venetian blinds; mosquito nets) for Fendi's eco-friendly line Carmina Campus. In true *agriturismo* tradition, the farm supplies much of the menu at the restaurant. Order the lemon-ricotta ravioli with pine-nut pesto; the shaved cheese on top comes courtesy of Fendi's flock of Sardinian sheep.

30 Via Giacomo Andreassi; 39-06/3089-6488; icasalidelpino.com. **$$**

Owner Ilaria Venturini Fendi with a few of her *agriturismo*'s residents.

Monastero Santa Rosa

In 1681, the Dominican sisters of Santa Rosa sought heaven on earth—and found it amid the lemon trees and lavender on a limestone cliff 600 feet above the Amalfi Coast. Now, the convent is a luxury hotel and labyrinthine spa, the pet project of American Bianca Sharma. The nuns' living quarters have been combined to create 20 spacious suites with vaulted ceilings and bougainvillea-clad balconies; each is filled with historic photographs and antiques collected during Sharma's travels. A monastic spirit endures in the 12th-century chapel and the two dozen herbs grown throughout the property, a tribute to the order's once-famous apothecary. Bliss of a more secular sort can be found during a warm wax-candle massage, or a swim in the infinity pool overhanging the Gulf of Salerno. The ultimate material indulgence: guests have access to a private helipad, a few houses away.

2 Via Roma, Conca dei Marini; 39-0898/321-199; monasterosantarosa.com. **$$$$**

Monastero Santa Rosa's terraced gardens and cliffside pool.

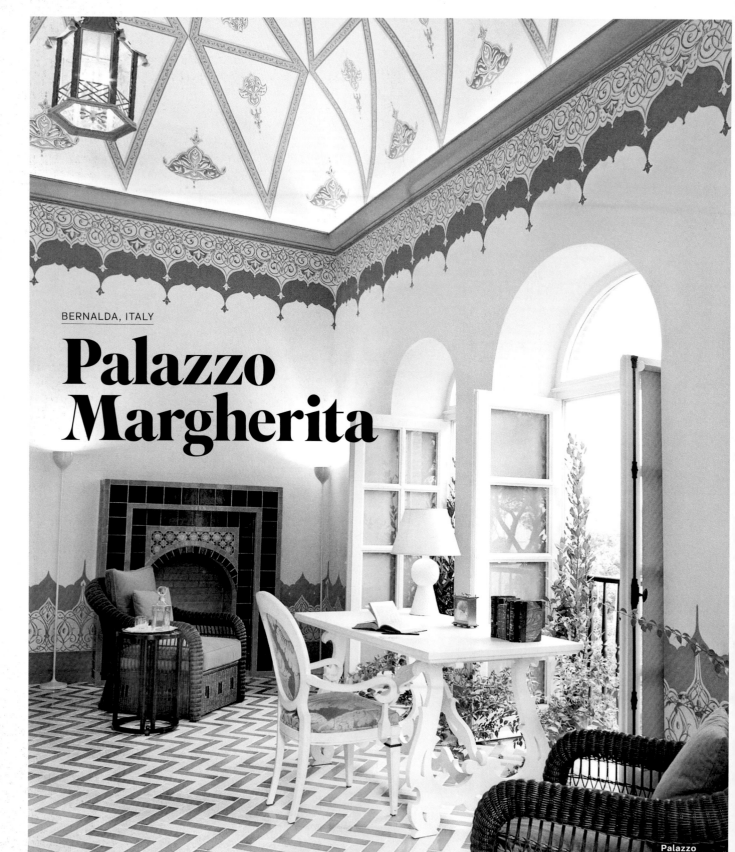

Palazzo Margherita

Palazzo Margherita's vibrant suite No. 9.

"*Bernalda bella.*" Those were the words Francis Ford Coppola's grandfather used to describe his birthplace—the hilltop village of Bernalda, Basilicata, in southern Italy. After several incursions into the Central American jungle, the *Godfather* director has gone back to his ancestral roots for his fifth property, the nine-room Palazzo Margherita. Among olive and grape groves near the Ionian Sea, the 19th-century Belle Époque estate was restored with the help of French designer Jacques Grange; suites feature *bejmat*-tiled floors, salvaged frescoes, claw-foot tubs, and Juliet balconies overlooking a courtyard garden. In the brick-vaulted kitchen, guests learn to cook regional dishes such as pappardelle with bread crumbs and tomatoes. There's also a screening room with a library of 300 classic Italian films—handpicked, naturally, by Coppola himself.

64 Corso Umberto; 39-0835/549-060; coppolaresorts.com. **$$$**

The villa's entrance courtyard.

Villa Tre Ville

Amid multilevel gardens that spill down toward the Mediterranean, opera and film director Franco Zeffirelli created his private refuge: a seaside estate where he entertained some of the biggest stars of stage and screen. It has since been converted into the 15-room Villa Tre Ville, but some of Zeffirelli's own design choices remain, including the original majolica floors and the mother-of-pearl bedroom furniture he brought back from a trip to Syria. Modern updates in the large suites—which have hosted the likes of Maria Callas, Leonard Bernstein, and Elizabeth Taylor—include star-shaped wall sconces and rain showers. From the property's jetty, a wooden motorboat whisks guests to nearby Amalfi Coast beaches. At dusk, *limoncello* is served under the vine-draped arbor, a prelude to meals that feel like elaborate dinner parties among friends. Almost everywhere you look, the bay is before you— a vision as cinematic as any of Zeffirelli's movie masterpieces.

30 Via Arienzo; 39-089/812-2411; villatreville.it. **$$$$$**

A terraced room at Villa Tre Ville, with a view to the sea.

The Hilton
Frankfurt Airport's
atrium lobby.

FRANKFURT, GERMANY

Hilton Frankfurt Airport

Airport hotels have always been necessary but unloved stopovers for the depleted traveler. The Hilton Frankfurt, however, is a destination unto itself, a stylish, hyper-connected oasis. Centrally located a short stroll from frenetic Terminal 1, the hotel comprises two stacks of rooms on either side of a sunlit atrium. The Hamburg-based interiors firm Joi added eye-catching touches like the low-slung Patricia Urquiola–designed chairs in the lobby and the leather-clad wardrobes in the bedrooms; a half-dozen orbs suspended from the atrium roof glow in different colors each evening. Adding to the thoughtfully curated ambience is a menu of German comfort food at the hotel's Rise restaurant (order the "local special," a Vogelsberger onion tart). This kind of cultural specificity is the last thing you expect at the airport—and that's precisely the point. You might even find yourself staying longer than a night.

The Squaire, Frankfurt Airport; 800/445-8667 or 49-69/2601-2000; hilton.com. $$

Arriving at the hotel and the surrounding Squaire complex.

A whimsical guest
room at Andaz
Amsterdam
Prinsengracht.

Andaz Amsterdam Prinsengracht

Renowned for his fantastical interiors, Netherlands-born designer Marcel Wanders does his hometown proud with the 122-room Andaz Amsterdam Prinsengracht. Surrounded by 18th-century canal houses in the Jordaan district, the onetime library now features Delft blues, nautical motifs, and oddly shaped custom furniture, redefining the building as both an ode to Holland's 17th-century charms and a hub for today's creative class. A walk through the lobby is like a journey down the rabbit hole. Chandeliers nestled in massive bells and luminous LED constellations hang inside a moonlit atrium worthy of Tim Burton's film version of *Alice in Wonderland*; a girl painted on the mural behind the Blue Spoon restaurant's garden could be Alice herself. Rooms are equally imaginative, with wallpapers depicting giant goldfish, one-of-a-kind sink basins hand-painted by Wanders, and cocoon-style chairs. In a city famous for open-mindedness, this is the perfect accommodation.

587 Prinsengracht; 800/875-5036 or 31-20/523-1234; andaz.com. **$$$**

A high-ceilinged
lounge area
at Hotel Julien.

The rooftop terrace overlooking Antwerp's Old Town. Below: Laying low in a guest room.

ANTWERP, BELGIUM

Hotel Julien

The Flemish have a knack for taking an area not much larger than an air shaft and transforming it into a sanctuary. Case in point: the Hotel Julien, a 21-room hideaway spread across two 19th-century buildings in Antwerp's old city. In both structures, walls of gridded glass open onto tidy green courtyards filled with asymmetrical waves of evergreen hedges, the work of celebrated landscape designer Jacques Wirtz. The blond-wood entry reveals an all-white foyer adorned with a simple domed light fixture, while modern sectionals in pale gray wool flank the parlor's twin black-marble fireplaces. Rooms are similarly sleek and spare, outfitted with Eames chairs, colorful wool throws atop crisp white beds, and works by local photographers. On warm afternoons, head up to the rooftop terrace to enjoy a Belgian brew in sight of the city's towering cathedral.

24 Korte Nieuwstraat; 32-3/229-0600; hotel-julien.com. **$$**

europe

Chambres d'Hôtes Hôtel Verhaegen

Rare are the places where you can experience the art in *l'art de vivre*. Rarer still is the hotel that makes you want to abandon the rest of your itinerary on arrival. Such is the four-room Hôtel Verhaegen, in a listed 18th-century *hôtel particulier* near Ghent's medieval Graslei district. Design duo Jan Rosseel and Marc Vergauwe knew what to enhance and when to leave well enough alone, retaining the architectural shell of the building while adding wit, comfort, and appropriately invisible technology. Shapely modern lamps offset boiserie and paintings by 18th-century Flemish artists; striped carpets on the stairs and in the bedrooms complement the original herringbone-wood and black-and-white marble floors. Even breakfast is a study in contrasts: guests can be served in either the grand Rococo dining room or the peaceful courtyard garden.

110 Oude Houtlei; 32-9/265-0760; hotelverhaegen.be. **$$**

Old-world details in one of Chambres d'Hôtes Hôtel Verhaegen's bedrooms.

Antiq Palace Hotel & Spa

Set on a quiet street in the Slovenian capital's Old Town, the 13-suite Antiq Palace Hotel & Spa is awash in the vestiges of its past. The palazzo was built for a well-placed Austrian family but fell into disrepair; now two locals have restored it for a new life. With thick walls and high ceilings—most of them still bearing their original frescoes—the hotel stays warm in the winter and cool in the summer, and the rooms are Immense and eccentrically homey in their décor (ornate upholstered armchairs counter such classic touches as French windows and blond-oak-parquet floors). Public spaces are a mix of courtyards and colonnades, with whitewashed walls and Art Deco sconces that set the scene for elegant alfresco dinners. Those lilting strains you hear are students honing their skills at one of the city's great music schools, located just a few hundred feet away.

10 Gosposka Ul.; 386/8389-6700; antiqpalace.com. **$**

A server in the hotel's coffee bar. Above: A whitewashed guest room.

Amanzo'e

Just when you thought there couldn't possibly be any more variations on the word *aman*, the trailblazing hotel company has opened Amanzo'e, straddling a hilltop in a remote area of Greece's Peloponnese peninsula. Architect Ed Tuttle's pared-down retreat strikes a balance between serenity and drama with tranquil reflecting pools and soaring marble walls. Walkways between the 38 pavilions are lined with fragrant lavender and rosemary bushes, and ample terraces off each suite look out onto the Argosaronic Gulf or the surrounding valley. True to the brand's style, every aspect of the property is tastefully done yet discreetly over-the-top: there's a tai chi and yoga studio with retractable floor-to-ceiling windows, two hammams in the spa, and a Mercedes SUV to ferry guests from the hotel to the private beach club five minutes away.

Porto Heli, Kranidi; 800/477-9180 or 30-275/477-2888; amanresorts.com. $$$$$

A look inside one of the guest pavilions at Amanzo'e.

Olive- and pine-forested hills beyond a private pool at Amanruya.

Amanruya

Come summer, Bodrum takes its place among the "it" capitals of the Mediterranean. The smart set has traditionally decamped at the stylish Maçakizi hotel, yet all that may be changing since Aman's Amanruya established itself above the Gulf of Mandalya. Inspired by Anatolian villages along Turkey's southern coast, the 50-acre resort has 36 cottages overlooking the Aegean, with Turkish charcoal barbecues and individual pools and gardens. The three-story library is stocked with tomes on the history of the Ottoman Empire, a theme echoed in the traditional dishes served in the four dining areas. An added thrill for culture buffs: the ancient ruins at Priene are within an hour's drive away.

Bülent Ecevit Çad.; 800/477-9180 or 90-252/311-1212; amanresorts.com. **$$$$$**

europe

A tented suite at Lamai Serengeti, in Tanzania's Serengeti National Park.

Africa+ The Middle East

A carved doorway at Le Jardin des Biehn. Above: The hotel's courtyard, with an entrance to its hammam.

Le Jardin des Biehn

After 30 years spent scouring the globe for rare and exquisite objects, French antiques collector Michel Biehn retreated to Fez's ancient medina to open a small hotel in what was once a pasha's summer palace. The result: Le Jardin des Biehn, with nine guest rooms that form an intoxicating whirl of textures and patterns. A crimson armoire from Sichuan is displayed near a concubine's chair from Beijing; a wall-size Uzbek tapestry sets off an 18th-century Persian mirror. Tying it all together are Moorish architectural details, including a courtyard framed by Moghul archways, walls inlaid with mosaic tiles, and a garden that provides ingredients for the hotel's Fez Café. Hicham, one of the chefs, moonlights as a maker of leather babouches, crafting the slippers to order in hues ranging from ocher to pale blue. Guests may also peruse the Islamic textiles in Biehn's on-site gallery—where, for a price, you can begin a collection of your own.

13 Akbat Sbaa, Douh; 212-6/6464-7679; jardindesbiehn.com. $

An antiques-filled
guest room on
the second floor.

163

Palais Namaskar

Palais Namaskar's pool and domed pavilions.

There's no shortage of ultrachic lodgings in Marrakesh, where every intimate new *riad* seems to out-design the last. Now the Oetker Collection—a pedigreed European hotel group with big expansion plans—is turning heads with the debut of Palais Namaskar, a grand getaway in the city's upscale Palmeraie neighborhood. Forty-one suites and villas, including two gold-domed palaces that come with butler service, are set on more than 12 acres of gardens and ponds edged by Moghul and Andalusian arches. The classic architecture belies the modern interiors, with their aubergine palettes, streamlined furnishings, and oblong fireplaces. You'll find the same sleek aesthetic in the hotel's 14-seat private jet, which whisks guests between Casablanca and Marrakesh in less than half an hour. Consider it a magic carpet for the 21st century.

88/69 Rte. de Bab Atlas; 212-524/299-800; palaisnamaskar.com. **$$$$**

The Selman

The Jacques
Garcia–designed
restaurant
at the Selman.

You've got to hand it to Jacques Garcia. The designer behind the 2009 revamp of Marrakesh's legendary La Mamounia has created yet another buzzy haven for the style set: the Se!man, a walled compound at the foot of the Atlas Mountains. The 62 guest rooms and 13,000-square-foot spa hark back to Morocco's golden age with *mashrabiya* screens, hand-made rugs, and a 260-foot reflecting pool, while ornate crystal chandeliers in the lobby nod to the city's French heritage. State-of-the-art stables reflect the owner's passion for Arabian horses (eight of which reside on the property). In the afternoon, as you sip tea on the shady veranda, the only sound breaking the silence will be that of hooves treading softly in the grassy paddock near your perch.

Km 5, Rte. d'Amizmiz; 212-524/459-600; selman-marrakech.com. **$$$$**

MARRAKESH, MOROCCO

Fellah Hotel

In the lush Ourika Valley, 20 minutes outside Marrakesh, the Fellah is an inspired concept: half hotel, half artists' colony. One building welcomes scholars-in-residence through a program partly funded by Libraries Without Borders, and another houses visiting international artists who collaborate on projects with local craftspeople. Hotel guests stay in 10 villas, in which 69 guest rooms steer clear of the usual *Arabian Nights* fantasy with sleek finishes, contemporary furnishings, and vintage photographs sourced from nearby souks. RSVP for the weekly Banquet de Fellah, at which guest philosophers, actors, and artists lead roundtable discussions inspired by Plato's *Symposium*. Food for thought: chef Olivier Dechaise serves innovative meals relating to the topic at hand.

Km 13, Rte. de l'Ourika; 212-525/065-000; fellah-hotel.com. **$$**

A swimming
pool backed by
the desert at
the Fellah Hotel.

A guest room at Sofitel Legend Old Cataract. Right: A corridor off the lobby.

ASWAN, EGYPT

Sofitel Legend Old Cataract

An hour's flight south of Cairo, Aswan saw glory in the 1950's, when politicos and boldfaced names arrived to visit the newly constructed Aswan Dam. Even now, it remains a bright spot in an area increasingly closed off to tourism, having kept out of the fray during Egypt's recent unrest. So the top-to-bottom renovation of the landmark Sofitel Legend Old Cataract comes as a welcome development. Of the hotel's two buildings, the Nile is the more modern, with walls of windows that frame the property's gardens. History buffs prefer the Palace, where Sofitel's preservation efforts are on full display in public spaces with Egyptian antiques, vintage furnishings, and Oriental rugs. What hasn't changed: the hotel's terrace, which still offers an inimitable view of the felucca boats that ply the river.

Abtal El Tahrir St.; 800/763-4835 or 20-97/231-6000; sofitel.com. **$$$**

The hotel's infinity pool, overlooking the Nile River.

Lamai Serengeti

The northwestern corner of the Serengeti was off-limits to development until recently, but a handful of safari companies have lately set up camp. By far the most arresting new property is Lamai, from the pioneering luxury outfitter Nomad Tanzania. Amid the ancient boulders of the Kogakuria Kopje, a natural rock swimming pool and 12 permanent thatched-roof tented suites (woven rugs; blond wood flooring; handblown glass lamps) blend seamlessly into the landscape. Thoughtful touches abound—each suite has a valet box where fresh coffee is delivered in time for your guided nature walk, and traditional bush dinners are served by torchlight under the stars. But Lamai's real attraction is that it provides unparalleled encounters with the Big Five, as well as sightings of the migrating herds of wildebeests that cross the nearby Mara River between July and October. This is the stuff that safari dreams are made of.

44-203/137-9905; nomad-tanzania.com; $4,300 per week, all-inclusive.

A thatched-roof lounge among the trees at Lamai Serengeti.

The Residence's
open-sided lobby.

ZANZIBAR, TANZANIA

The Residence

The Indian Ocean laps against a mile-long beach at the Residence, the centerpiece of an 80-acre estate on Zanzibar's southwestern coast. The 66 understated villas hint at the area's African and Middle Eastern heritage with carved furnishings and handwoven linens; plunge pools and contemporary artwork keep quarters rooted in the present. Sip sunset cocktails on a jetty that stretches 450 feet into the sea, then try one of the *shisha* pipes in the bar before dining on Swahili dishes made with the spices that established the island as an important stop on ancient trade routes. See them at their source— and gain a deeper understanding of Zanzibar's cultural traditions—on a tour of the farms where fragrant cloves, pepper, and nutmeg are harvested.

Mchamgamle, Kizimkazi; 255-24/555-5000; theresidence.com. **$$$$$**

africa + the middle east

ZANZIBAR, TANZANIA

Mashariki Palace Hotel

Muted tones in one of the guest rooms at Mashariki Palace Hotel. Opposite: An intricate entranceway in the former palace.

The call to prayer rings throughout the Mashariki Palace Hotel, a converted 19th-century residence ensconced within the winding streets of Stone Town. Eighteen whitewashed rooms are the embodiment of Swahili architecture, with ornately carved door frames, stone columns, and stucco embrasures. A rooftop terrace offers sunset views of the ocean, and a cool inner courtyard provides a tranquil place to enjoy cardamom-spiced tea. The hotel's central location gives you easy access to the nearby House of Wonders—another palace, now a museum dedicated to East Africa's multiethnic culture. And no visitor should miss a stroll through the busy night market at Forodhani Gardens, where vendors cook regional specialties as breezes blow in from the sea.

Forodhani, Chumba ya moto 293; 255-24/223-7232; masharikipalacehotel.com. **$$**

LIVINGSTONE, ZAMBIA

Tongabezi Lodge

A symphony of grunting hippos and chortling baboons supplies the sound track for your stay at Tongabezi Lodge, a collection of thatched-roof cottages on an isolated bank of the Zambezi River. Perfectly sited for game drives and bush walks, the hotel offers exactly what you'd expect from a sybaritic safari outpost, including personal valets, four-poster beds, and private plunge pools; during full moons, guides lead guests to witness lunar rainbows over nearby Victoria Falls. Equally impressive are the lodge's far-reaching humanitarian efforts: what began as a preschool for the staff's children now enrolls 198 students and has produced national champions in poetry and dance. And many students have gone on to attend high school in neighboring Livingstone, thanks to sponsorships from Tongabezi guests.

260-213/327-450; tongabezi.com; all-inclusive. **$$$$**

Tongabezi Lodge's Lookout Lounge, on the Zambezi River.

A smoked-salmon sandwich served at Olive Exclusive. Left: The Erongo Suite.

Olive Exclusive

Long known as a post-safari stopover from Namibia's wildlife-rich national parks, Windhoek had little in the way of truly stylish sanctuaries. Enter the Olive Exclusive, the city's first contemporary boutique hotel, set in a quiet residential neighborhood a five-minute drive from the center of town. Designed by South African photographer Micky Hoyle, each of the seven suites is inspired by a different Namibian region: Erongo, for example, is named for a ring of mountains in the heart of the country and is done up in earthy tones, with sculptural woven ceiling lights and larger-than-life photographs by Hoyle on the walls. Ample modern conveniences—in-room laptops; deep soaking tubs; a plunge pool flanked by silvery olive trees—are all the more appreciated after an adventure in Namibia's otherworldly desert landscape.

22 Promenaden St.; 264-61/239-199; theolive-namibia.com. **$$$**

A photographic
mural in the
Otavi Suite's
dining area.

White Pearl Resorts Ponta Mamoli

A sandy, lantern-lit lounge at White Pearl Resorts Ponta Mamoli.

The only hotel for miles on Mozambique's untouched southern shore, the White Pearl is the first part of a master plan to open up this poor but wildly beautiful area to sustainable tourism. Your respite begins with a 30-minute helicopter ride from the capital city of Maputo. Amid the dunes, 22 stand-alone oceanside suites await with warm wood furnishings and crisp organic linens in muted shades of sand and sea. The area is rife with epic experiences—you can gallop on horseback along the vast golden beach or visit an offshore reef to see turtles, dolphins, and humpback whales among vividly colored coral formations. Back on land, a well-made mojito at the chic beach bar gives a hint of the direction in which this pristine coastline is heading.

27-35/592-8100; whitepearlresorts.com. **$$$$**

Abu Dhabi, U.A.E.

For years, Abu Dhabi stood in the shadow of its high-profile neighbor Dubai. But now, flush with 95 percent of the U.A.E.'s oil, the lesser-known emirate is building its own iconic skyline—and reshaping the capital city's image from a business center to a cultural hub for the modern Middle East. No less inspiring is the bevy of upscale resorts, many of them architectural landmarks in their own right.

ARABIAN GULF

PORT ZAYED

LULU ISLAND

SAADIYAT ISLAND

SHEIKH KHALIFA BIN ZAYED ST.

CORNICHE

AL REEM ISLAND

1 Park Hyatt

On Saadiyat Island, a seven-minute drive from downtown, the Park Hyatt is a peaceful retreat bordered by five miles of protected turtle-nesting habitat. Courtyards and marble-lined public spaces lead to 306 contemporary rooms with oak floors and freestanding bathtubs; private balconies look onto the Persian Gulf and the hotel's swimming pool. The two-story Atarmia Spa is *the* place for shiatsu facial massages and deep-tissue rubdowns. Afterward, join well-heeled Emiratis for drinks by the 80-foot lap pool.

877/875-4658; park.hyatt.com. $$

The main pool at the Park Hyatt, on Saadiyat Island.

St. Regis's 55th & 5th, The Grill restaurant.

In the lobby of the Rocco Forte Hotel.

2 St. Regis

On the same stretch of sand as the Park Hyatt, the cream-colored St. Regis features Arabia-meets–Art Deco décor that pays homage to both the Persian Gulf and the brand's New York origins. An 18-hole golf course overlooks miles of white shoreline, and at 55th & 5th, The Grill—the signature restaurant named for the brand's Manhattan flagship—a multicultural menu is anchored by prime cuts of grass-fed beef, all aged with Himalayan rock salt a minimum of 21 days. The 377-room hotel is nothing if not well placed; more big things are coming to Saadiyat Island, including outposts of both the Louvre (2015) and the Guggenheim (2017).

877/787-3447; st.regis.com. **$$**

3 Rocco Forte Hotel

The exterior of the European luxury brand's first Middle Eastern property is a bit more whimsical than the rest of the hotels on the scene. Wavy blue-and-green glass mirrors the colors of the Gulf; interiors come courtesy of designer Olga Polizzi, who incorporated work by regional artists throughout the hotel. Each of the 281 rooms has sleek marble-and-limestone bathrooms and modern Arabian motifs (*mashrabiya*-style latticework screens; colorful mosaics). But it's the sweeping views from the Blue Bar, suspended in the middle of an 11-story atrium, that have guests gawking—and returning.

Sheikh Rashid Bin Saeed Al Maktoum St.; 888/667-9477; roccofortehotels.com. **$$**

A room high above Dubai at the JW Marriott Marquis.

JW Marriott Marquis

Briefcase-toting road warriors have a new stomping ground in the 1,164-foot-high JW Marriott Marquis, the tallest hotel in the world. But here they can play as hard as they work. The shimmering twin towers house a staggering number of diversions: 1,608 streamlined rooms with floor-to-ceiling windows facing the Dubai skyline; a 72nd-floor cigar lounge; and a dazzling spa with treatments that incorporate mud from the Dead Sea. British-based chef Atul Kochhar has opened his first Middle Eastern venture—an Indian restaurant serving such dishes as heirloom tomatoes topped with fennel crisps and spiced fried chicken with curry leaves—alongside eight other restaurants and five cocktail bars and lounges perfect for late-night revelry. Just don't forget to arrange a wake-up call for your morning meeting.

Sheikh Zayed Rd.; 888/236-2427 or 971-4/414-0000; jwmarriott.com. **$$**

ACRE, ISRAEL

Efendi Hotel

In the beach-lined port city of Acre, in Israel's northern Galilee, a pair of Ottoman-era mansions sat empty for years until local restaurateur Uri Jeremias saw their untapped potential. Under his watchful eye—and in strict accordance with Israel's Antiquities Authority guidelines—the two residences, complete with Byzantine walls and Crusader-period cellars, were intricately restored to become the palatial Efendi Hotel. The 12 white-on-white rooms are paragons of preservation, with marble floors and the original trompe l'oeil ceilings. In lieu of turndown chocolates, guests indulge in handmade Arab sweets presented in silver boxes. Israeli wines and pan-Mediterranean dishes are the focus in the 900-year-old cellar turned tapas bar; after you've had your fill, stroll south along the Mediterranean, passing the city's 4,000-year-old sights along the way.

Louis IX St.; 972-747/299-799; efendi-hotel.com. **$$**

One of the property's three light-filled lobbies.

A server at Sofitel So's
Park Society
Restaurant & Bar,
which overlooks the
Bangkok skyline.

Asia

A sunlit seating area in the Palace Lounge.

TOKYO

Palace Hotel

In the shadow of the Imperial Palace, a storied 1961 property is once again channeling its understated opulence. Thanks to the skillful eye of Australian interior designer Terry McGinnity, the revamped Palace Hotel evokes the natural beauty of the royal residence's serene outer gardens in 290 earth-toned guest rooms with leafy motifs, deep green carpets, and floor-to-ceiling windows. Traditional Japanese touches abound throughout, from the kimono-clad servers in the lobby café to the cast-iron teapots in suites. Nearby, a terrace doubles as an alfresco *salon de thé,* where you can choose from 48 blends with the park's fountains as a meditative backdrop. It's all part of a $1.2 billion development that includes Japan's first Evian spa, a high-end subterranean shopping center, and 10 restaurants from some of the country's most celebrated chefs. Have the emperors ever had it so good?

1-1-1 Marunouchi, Chiyoda-ku; 800/223-6800 or 81-3/3211-5211; palacehoteltokyo.com. **$$$$**

The pool at the complex's Evian Spa Tokyo. Above: Neutral hues in a Park suite.

Andaz

In a city in the midst of a hotel boom, standing out is no small feat. Yet Andaz Shanghai—the Asian debut for Hyatt's boutique brand—pulls it off with a fresh and stylish vibe. A collaboration between U.S.-based architectural group Kohn Pedersen Fox and Japanese interiors firm Super Potato, the hotel combines playful elements (a coffee lounge cocooned inside an egg-shaped steel sculpture suspended above the lobby) and guest-friendly touches (in-room mini-bar snacks are free of charge). Curved, retro-space-age windows in the 307 rooms provide bang-on views of the surrounding Xintiandi district and the pulsing neon heart of Shanghai. And if you're wondering why the staff looks so spiffy, it's because their chic black ensembles were designed by native daughter Han Feng, whose work ranges from couture collections to costumes for New York's Metropolitan Opera.

88 Songshan Rd.; 877/875-5036 or 86-21/2310-1234; andaz.com. **$$$**

Andaz Shanghai's honeycomb-like exterior. Left: Breakfast in the hotel's Hai Pai restaurant.

The Brew bar at the Kerry Hotel Pudong.

Kerry Hotel Pudong

Never mix business and pleasure? Whoever said that hasn't stayed at the Kerry Hotel, the flagship property of Shangri-La's new lifestyle brand. Here, the seasoned Hong Kong–based hotel group offers all the amenities to keep hard-core business travelers happy (round-the-clock corporate facilities; easy train access from the airport; private offices for rent) while amping up the fun factor (try the martial-arts-inspired wushu body therapy in the spa). Upstairs, the 574 guest suites are filled with natural light and feature streamlined furnishings with warm wood accents. And the Kerry has China's largest hotel gym—more than 64,500 square feet of exercise space. But whether you're brokering a deal or kicking back after touring the frenetic Pudong neighborhood, you'll definitely want to book a table at the Brew, where New Zealand–born Leon Mickelson handcrafts his addictive, coriander-infused Belgian-style beer.

1388 Hua Mu Rd.; 866/565-5050 or 86-21/6169-8888; thekerryhotels.com. **$$$**

asia

197

The Jervois

The slim glass tower of the Jervois, designed by French architect Florent Nédélec.

The 36-story Jervois offers a welcome respite from the chockablock clamor of the up-and-coming Sheung Wan district. Although the elevator delivers you into a cubbyhole of a private lobby, the burled-wood door to your apartment-style suite reveals a surprisingly airy monochromatic space, created by French designer Christian Liaigre. Features include a fully equipped kitchen and a small dining area, a marble-clad bathroom, and a wall of windows that all but invite the skyline inside. Cushy leather-framed beds done up in Frette linens and goose-down pillows provide a soft landing after a day spent negotiating the streets of Hong Kong. Before you call it a night, however, head to Yardbird, a not-so-secret *izakaya* five minutes away, and order a batch of savory beak-to-tail yakitori chicken skewers.

89 Jervois St.; 852/3994-9000; thejervois.com. **$$**

Inside one of the property's apartment-style guest rooms.

A Premium
Indulgence suite
at Vivanta
by Taj-Bekal.

KAPPIL BEACH, INDIA

Vivanta by Taj-Bekal

The tropical backwaters of Kerala, in southwestern India, are getting a dose of luxury thanks to the Vivanta by Taj - Bekal, a sprawling new spa retreat. The hotel's lush environs—where the Kappil River meets the Arabian Sea—are reflected throughout the 26-acre property: flowing contours and coir-and-thatch façades mimic the region's famous Kettuvallam houseboats, while the 71 rooms (many opening onto private plunge pools) are painted with murals inspired by Hindu mythology. For an inside look at Kerala's food scene, chef Valentine will take you on a "fish walk" to the nearby Pallikera market—an experience enriched by his extensive knowledge of local aquaculture. Of course, the cornerstone of the hotel is the 165,000-square-foot Jiva spa, which focuses on rejuvenating aromatherapy and ayurvedic treatments, the most thorough course of which lasts a full two weeks. Better start clearing your calendar.

866/969-1825 or 91-46/7661-6612; vivantabytaj.com. $

Raas, Jodhpur

The alleyways of Jodhpur's ancient walled city are too narrow for cars, but guests at the Raas need not fret: a vintage-style auto-rickshaw awaits to take you to the hotel's imposing grand archway. Beyond, a shaded courtyard is surrounded by a 300-year-old red sandstone *haveli*, where 39 minimalist rooms combine traditional elements (latticed screens and chandeliers) with sleek touches such as black terrazzo floors and deep soaking tubs. At the restaurant, authentic Rajasthani dishes are made with organic vegetables grown nearby. Moghul-style gardens complete the scene, along with dazzling vistas of the 15th-century Mehrangarh desert fort—a stone's throw away.

A suite balcony at Raas, Jodhpur, with a view of the surrounding walled city.

Makrana Mohalla; 91-291/263-6455; raasjodhpur.com. $

The pool area, backed by the hotel's contemporary sandstone façade.

The Maldives

Searching for the next great escape? Set a course for the Maldives, where sybaritic resorts are popping up on even the most far-flung atolls. It takes time and an adventurous spirit to reach this archipelago of 1,192 islands in the Indian Ocean: your (invariably long) flight is followed by a seaplane or speedboat ride from the capital, Male, or the neighboring port, Hulhule. Here, six retreats that make the journey worthwhile.

INDIAN OCEAN

SHAVIYANI ATOLL

BAA ATOLL

1

2

SOUTH MALE ATOLL

3

DHAALU ATOLL

4

LAAMU ATOLL

ONE AND A HALF DEGREE CHANNEL

6

5

HUVADHOO ATOLL

EQUATOR

1 Dusit Thani

This Thai-style resort is an ideal base from which to explore the Baa Atoll and the colorful reefs of Hanifaru Huraa, part of a UNESCO World Biosphere Reserve. Let the resident marine biologist point out whale sharks and mantas on a guided tour, or retire to one of the 20 Balau-teak villas set over a blue lagoon (80 others are situated throughout the grounds). Prefer an even more pampered experience? You'll find the spa in a quiet coconut grove.

Mudhoo Island; 011-960/660-8888; dusit.com. **$$$$$**

Dusit Thani's overwater restaurant and villas.

A Beach villa and private pool at Jumeirah Vittaveli.

The Edge restaurant at Niyama.

2 Jumeirah Vittaveli

Only a 20-minute boat ride from the airport, the Jumeirah occupies a pristine swath of white sand on a nearby isle in the South Male Atoll. The eco-focused getaway serves as a template for responsible enterprise in the region: the hotel sponsors a local school system, selling the children's paintings at an on-site gallery, and heats water using the exhaust from its generators, reducing its carbon footprint. The setting is undeniably sumptuous—witness the five Lagoon suites, which are situated 300 feet from the mainland and have 24-hour butler service. Not to miss: sunset drinks on the deck at the waterfront Fenesse restaurant.

Bolifushi Island; 877/854-8051 or 011-960/664-2020; jumeirah.com. $$$$$

3 Niyama

At this 86-suite resort on the Dhaalu Atoll, the focus is on unbridled luxury· on arrival you're assigned a personal butler who can both fill your bath and arrange a snorkeling cruise aboard a traditional dhoni sailboat. Stone paths from some of the rooms lead to private outdoor showers. Each public space outshines the last. There's a torchlit, safari-camp-style restaurant that serves entrées grilled over open flames; a spa nestled within an orchard of leafy lime trees; and a bar that's accessible only by boat. But the standout has to be the below-sea-level nightclub, where DJ's burn up the dance floor beneath the waves.

Embudhufushi and Olhuveli Islands; 011-960/676-2828; peraquum.com. $$$$$

A teak guest
suite at
Six Senses
Laamu.

4 Six Senses Laamu

It doesn't get any
more secluded than the
eco-luxe Six Senses,
the Laamu Atoll's only
resort. The 97 thatched-
roof villas have mesh
hammocks splayed over
the tide and glass tubs
that allow you to peer in
on schools of parrot
fish. Head out with the
surf coach for a lesson on
an eight-foot reef break
called Yin Yang, just
offshore—but be back
in time for a dinner of
grilled reef fish served in
your villa. The night
ends with a stargazing
session led by the hotel's
resident astronomer.

*Olhuveli Island;
011-960/980-0800;
sixsenses.com.* **$$$$**

A pool area at the Park Hyatt Maldives Hadahaa.

5 The Residence

After opening resorts in Tunis, Mauritius, and Zanzibar, the Singapore-based brand set its sights on the remote Huvadhoo Atoll. All manner of aquatic diversions are available, from deep-sea fishing to catamaran sailing lessons. Yet the real draw lies in the 94 subdued villas, which showcase the natural beauty of the islands with furniture made from local wood, muted handwoven fabrics, and 360-degree views of the azure expanse that surrounds you. A hammock on your private patio provides a perfect spot for relaxation, as do the six pavilions at the Clarins spa—located at the end of its own jetty.

Falhumaafushi Island; 011-960/682-0088; theresidence.com. **$$$$$**

6 Park Hyatt Maldives Hadahaa

Also in the Huvadhoo, the Park Hyatt offers a Modernist take on this far-off idyll. Fifty villas are elegantly spare: native timber and stone floors are serene but not sterile; technology is discreet yet effective (the Wi-Fi—should you have use for it—is complimentary); and sunlight floods the space, keeping the spotlight on cerulean panoramas. Outside, a lounge with spectacular sunset views calls to mind a traditional dhoni, the work of local shipbuilders. And a top-tier PADI program offers diving expeditions in search of rare whale sharks, hawksbill turtles, and eagle rays.

Hadahaa Island; 877/875-4658 or 011-960/682-1234; park.hyatt.com. **$$$$$**

A shaded
courtyard at
Villa Bentota.

BENTOTA, SRI LANKA

Villa Bentota

Forty years ago, Sri Lankan architect Geoffrey Bawa turned a decrepit 1880's villa on the beach-lined southern coast into the country's first boutique hotel. More recently, the 15-room property was reimagined by native design guru Shanth Fernando, who renamed it Villa Bentota and added his signature black-and-white stripes to the interiors. The public spaces are especially inviting—frangipani-fringed courtyards, a pool in a shaded garden, and a gallery space filled with works by local artists. Chef Nishantha Liyanage serves up traditional black pork curry and wasabi-crusted salmon at the hotel's streamlined Villa Café, housed in an open-air pavilion. The only thing between you and the beach is an antique railroad track, on which every so often an old locomotive rumbles by with waving passengers on their way to the port town of Galle.

138/18-138/22 Galle Rd.; 94-34/227-5311; paradiseroadhotels.com. **$$**

asia

BANGKOK

Sofitel So

A mural-size map of Bangkok at the Sofitel So.

210

A guest room that looks out on Lumphini Park.

High style meets cutting-edge technology at the Asian-Pacific debut of Sofitel's contemporary So brand. A kaleidoscopic mobile of fantastical creatures, created by Christian Lacroix, dominates the slate-colored lobby; the French designer is also behind the staff's fashion-forward uniforms. Upstairs, many of the 238 rooms—inspired by the Chinese elements of fire, water, earth, and metal—are well equipped for the next generation of plugged-in travelers, with in-suite iPads, Mac Minis, and free Wi-Fi. Guest room windows overlook either Lumphini Park or the buzzing streets of Sathorn, the downtown business district, which has become a favored nighttime haunt for the see-and-be-seen crowd. The same can be said for the So's rooftop bar, where a private area lined with moonlit cabanas is one of the most exclusive spots in town.

2 N. Sathorn Rd.; 800/763-4835 or 66-2/624-0000; sofitel.com. **$**

asia

The Mandarin Oriental Bangkok's pool, located across the Chao Phraya River from the hotel.

Porters in the hotel's lobby. Left: An Author's Heritage suite.

Mandarin Oriental

Check in at the Mandarin Oriental, on the Chao Phraya River, and you'll be in good company: Joseph Conrad, Graham Greene, and Noël Coward all stayed here during its heyday. Now the legendary 1879 hotel has entered a new phase with the completion of a much-anticipated face-lift. Tech amenities such as iPod docking stations and flat-screen TV's were added in the 393 rooms, along with more traditional details, including hand-tufted rugs and teak writing desks. Your personal butler can arrange a prime table for dim sum at the 1930's-inspired China House while you hop the private ferry to reach the Oriental's garden pool and spa across the river. Make time for the Moroccan-style *rhassoul*-mud steam bath—about as far from old Siam as you can get, but no one's complaining.

Soi 40, Charoenkrung Rd.; 800/526-6566 or 66-2/659-9000; mandarinoriental.com. **$$$**

asia

213

貸
殖
無

資
品
譜

鄂哇公司大寶行新張誌慶

BANGKOK

The Siam

Thai rock star and actor Krissada Sukosol Clapp can now add hotelier to his résumé. His Dusit neighborhood property comes off as a living museum, brimming with 19th-century maps of Siam and Art Deco curios from the performer's extensive collection (copper clocks; teak dressers; vintage luggage cases). Set in an interconnecting series of modern structures, the hotel is home to a first-rate spa and yoga terrace, a library, and 39 spacious guest rooms with king beds and deep soaking tubs. After being ferried down the Chao Phraya River and reassembled on site, three century-old traditional houses—in which glamorous Anglo-Thai socialite Connie Mangskau once entertained the likes of Jackie Kennedy and William Holden—have become an authentic Thai restaurant and cooking school. If all this sounds a little too tame for you, not to worry: there's a *Muay Thai* kickboxing center on the grounds as well.

3/2 Khao Rd.; 66-2/206-6999; thesiamhotel.com. **$$$$**

214

Asian Art Deco accents in a Courtyard Pool villa at the Siam.

A berry dessert from the restaurant at 137 Pillars House. Below: A soaking tub in a guest suite.

CHIANG MAI, THAILAND

137 Pillars House

Chiang Mai's reputation as the lower-key antidote to energetic Bangkok got a major boost with the opening of this tranquil, 30-suite retreat. While other boutique properties here have a tendency to out-hip one another, 137 Pillars House strikes an entirely different note: that of a gracious colonial residence. Located in a leafy neighborhood near the Mae Ping River, the two-acre property was once part of the sprawling compound of a British teak-trading company. A beautifully restored 19th-century bungalow now houses a library filled with books on Thai history and architecture as well as a lounge where afternoon tea is served daily. In the guest rooms, era-appropriate details include vintage-tiled verandas (with cane shades for added privacy) and rattan planter's chairs, as well as outdoor showers surrounded by tropical gardens. Even the discreetly attentive service evokes a more genteel time.

2 Soi 1, Nawatgate Rd.; 800/525-4800 or 66-53/247-788; 137pillarshouse.com. **$$$**

Afternoon tea in the property's stately garden.

asia

217

Song Saa Private Island

Exploring the necklace of pristine atolls off Cambodia's southeastern coast once meant a bumpy three-hour boat ride and bare-bones lodging. That all changed with the arrival of Song Saa, an ultra-luxe resort on two private islands. In just 30 minutes, guests are transported by speedboat from the port city of Sihanoukville to its white-sand shores; before you so much as step onto the dock, the staff greets you by name and offers a 15-minute foot massage, a hint at the deep relaxation to come. When you're not unwinding in one of the 27 beachfront villas, with their thatched roofs and weathered timber floors, you can swim near a protected reef and tour the resort's smaller island to the north, a nature reserve operated in conjunction with the national government. And even if you're not the spiritual type, a visit to the pagoda on the nearby island of Koh Rong to receive a blessing from local monks is a once-in-a-lifetime experience.

Koh Ouen; songsaa.com. **$$$$$**

A speedboat
view of Song Saa
Private Island.

SUMBA, INDONESIA

Nihiwatu

Some 400 miles east of Bali, Sumba is as off-the-radar as you can get. Home to one of the last animist cultures on earth, the island also harbors the world's most clandestine surf break—and with it, an eco-minded beachfront hideaway that's transforming this blissful place into a model of community outreach. On 588 acres that encompass ivory sand, verdant rice paddies, and dense jungle, the 12 luxury bungalows at Nihiwatu were built by local craftsmen and outfitted with handmade artifacts; electricity comes courtesy of biodiesel made from coconuts on site. That's not all: after raising more than $4 million in donations, the resort has built five health clinics (reducing cases of malaria in the area by 85 percent) and supplied clean water to more than 18,000 people via new wells and water stations. The result is a guilt-free harmony between island residents and visitors, who are only too happy to help.

Desa Hobawawi, West Sumba; 62-361/757-149; nihiwatu.com; all-inclusive. **$$$$$**

A lantern-lit path to Nihiwatu's restaurant. Left: Handwoven fabrics in one of the guest rooms.

An aerial view of
the Berkeley River
Lodge, in western
Australia's
Kimberley region.

Australia, New Zealand + The South Pacific

Afternoon tea at Blue Sydney's Water Bar.

Blue

Don't be fooled by the gingerbread-trimmed façade—Blue Sydney is more big-city cool than seaside classic. On a former shipping wharf at the eastern edge of Sydney Harbour, the industrial-chic hotel (the Taj Group's first Australian property) manages to feel both removed from the bustle of downtown and at the center of the action. The 100 loft-style rooms are streamlined and modern, many with soaring, girder-supported ceilings and windows that look out on the boats passing in the bay. On arrival, drop your bags and head straight to Water Bar, where scenesters sip martinis under atrium skylights. You might even find Russell Crowe snacking on canapés at the sumptuously cushioned lounge: the Aussie leading man lives right down the dock.

6 Cowper Wharf Rd.; 866/969-1825 or 61-2/9331-9000; tajhotels.com. **$$**

The exterior of the hotel, set on the Finger Wharf on Woolloomooloo Bay.

Hilton

When business travelers come to town, they hole up at the 43-story Hilton Sydney, a glass tower designed by the architects behind the Opera House's historic makeover. Casual visitors have good reason to join them. A quick walk from most major landmarks, the 579-room hotel exudes urban sophistication. A striking aluminum sculpture by Bronwyn Oliver spirals down four stories into the cavernous lobby; at the Tony Chi–designed Glass Brasserie, native chef Luke Mangan earns raves for his inventive dishes, including double-baked Gruyère soufflé and sashimi with ginger and Persian feta (pair it with one of the 900 varieties of wine on the menu). And the subterranean Marble, a Victorian-style bar that turns into a live music venue on weekends, is one of the most happening spots in town.

488 George St.; 800/445-8667 or 61-2/9266-2000; hilton.com. **$$**

Vine, a sculpture
by Australian artist
Bronwyn Oliver, in
Hilton Sydney's lobby.

The Langham

The Presidential
Suite at
the Langham
Melbourne.

With the charm of a small community and the worldliness of a modern metropolis, Melbourne has long been one of the most livable cities on the planet. Nowhere is this more apparent than in Southbank, a once-gritty Yarra River port that has morphed into a youthful, arty enclave. Base yourself at the 387-room Langham, the neighborhood's grande dame, which has ornate Waterford crystal chandeliers and Victorian-style furnishings. The 11,400-square-foot Chuan Spa features treatments inspired by traditional Chinese principles of yin and yang, as well as an indoor saltwater pool ideal for the famously unpredictable weather. Culture lovers, take note: steps from the hotel, the Arts Centre hosts the Melbourne Symphony Orchestra at its gleaming new concert hall, while a few blocks away, the National Gallery of Victoria—the region's oldest museum—displays a vast collection of international works.

1 Southgate Ave.; 800/588-9141 or 61-3/8696-8888; langhamhotels.com. **$$**

The panorama from the suite's private balcony.

The Kimberley, Australia

The rust-colored landscape of northwestern Oz remains as wild as it gets—one of the last frontiers in a country known for having more than its share of rugged corners. Until recently, few ventured into the remote territory of the Kimberley, which has some 2,000 miles of virgin coastline as well as caves with 40-millennia-old Aboriginal paintings. Now luxury camps have taken hold in the region, raising its profile among rustic-chic aesthetes.

TIMOR SEA

1

DRYSDALE RIVER NATIONAL PARK

2 3 KUNUNURRA RTE 1

GREGORY NATIONAL PARK

1 Berkeley River Lodge

An hour-long flight from Kununurra is the best way to reach the Berkeley River Lodge, a 20-villa hideaway with hardwood floors and freestanding tubs on the Joseph Bonaparte Gulf. Anglers have access to the area's pristine waterways, while nature enthusiasts can take expert-guided hikes to spot rock wallabies. Gourmet meals fit for a modern-day explorer await at the lodge's elegant dining room; don't miss the oak-smoked salmon flown in from Tasmania.

61-8/9169-1330; berkeleyriver.com.au. $$$$

The main house and pool area at Berkeley River Lodge.

Inside one of Home Valley Station's Grass Castle villas.

The expansive grounds at El Questro Homestead.

☷ Home Valley Station

If Home Valley Station looks familiar, that's because Hugh Jackman and Nicole Kidman shot scenes for the 2008 epic *Australia* here. The working ranch—which is held in trust by the Indigenous Land Corporation and fosters sustainable partnerships for native title landholders—still offers movie tours of key sites, but cinematic vistas are everywhere you turn. Activities run the gamut: the staff can arrange for an easy gorge walk or fishing expedition, or you can try your hand in a real cattle muster. At night, bed down in tents and villas scattered among boab and eucalyptus trees throughout the 615,000-acre parcel.

61-2/8296-8010; hvstation.com.au; all-inclusive. **$$**

☷ El Questro Homestead

The spirit of adventure pervades every inch of El Questro, a six-room refuge set on a million (yes, *million*) acres. Even dining outdoors is an exhilarating experience: a candlelit table clings to the edge of a 200-foot-deep ravine trolled by crocs. Dishes of fresh barramundi or western Australian lamb distract the vertigo-prone. Activities are equally adrenaline-pumping—take a helicopter tour of the cave systems above El Questro Gorge. Or choose relaxation and head to nearby Zebedee Springs, a series of natural thermal pools where you can soak in seclusion, out of sight of even the nosiest kangaroo.

El Questro Wilderness Park; 61-3/9426-7550; elquestro.com.au. **$$$**

Midcentury
accents
in the lounge
at Ohtel.

A platform bed in one of the hotel's guest rooms. Above: Ohtel's modern façade.

WELLINGTON, NEW ZEALAND

Ohtel

Energized by a booming film industry, New Zealand's capital has become a bastion of rough-hewn sophistication. Fashionable urbanites have a place to stay between more rugged pursuits: Ohtel, a boutique property built into a cliff near Wellington's inner harbor. Owner Alan Blundell outfitted 10 tech-savvy rooms with Midcentury Modern furnishings culled from flea markets and galleries, and installed solar panels on the roof. (A warning to the modest: bathrooms are separated from sleeping areas only by a glass partition and an opaque curtain.) On sunny days, it seems the whole city rushes to the waterfront. Join them on a stroll to nearby Te Papa, the New Zealand national museum, passing a parade of runners, bikers, and skateboarders along the way.

66 Oriental Parade; 64-4/803-0600; ohtel.com. **$$$**

australia, new zealand + the south pacific

Minaret Station

A starry night at
Minaret Station,
in New Zealand's
Southern Alps.

New Zealand's Southern Alps are one of the planet's last untouched landscapes. With the arrival of the region's first luxury camp, you no longer need be a celebrity or a hobbit (Peter Jackson filmed *The Lord of the Rings* here) to experience these snowcapped mountains and pristine lakes in style—though you will have to pay a premium. Minaret Station, a stone lodge with just four tented suites, is set on 65,000 acres of valley floor that can be reached from Queenstown only by helicopter. Amenities reflect the surroundings, from the sheepskin rugs to the bedside bottled water that comes from a nearby waterfall. A typical day might include a chopper ride to the belly of the Mount Aspiring glacier or, in summer, an expedition to the coast to dive for abalone and crayfish. If the fresh air doesn't lull you to sleep, a dip in your veranda's heated soaking tub should do the trick.

64-3/443-5860; minaretstation.com. **$$$$$**

A thatched-roof villa at Les Relais de Joséphine.

RANGIROA, FRENCH POLYNESIA

Les Relais de Joséphine

"Island time" takes on new meaning on Rangiroa, in French Polynesia's Tuamotu Archipelago, where the intimate Les Relais de Joséphine lets you while away the days care-free. The vision of Parisian Denise Caroggio, seven thatched-roof bungalows are furnished with four-poster beds draped in mosquito netting and reproductions of French-colonial antiques; three have large terraces that look out on the Tiputa Pass, the meeting point of the lagoon and the Pacific. At dawn, you may glimpse dolphins leaping from the water ahead of the incoming tide. The view is equally distracting come lunchtime at the French-inspired Le Dauphin Gourmand restaurant (order the curried shellfish). On your agenda, should you choose: a deep-sea boating trip with local fishermen or excursions to see the baby blacktip shark nursery at nearby Blue Lagoon.

Ohotu, Avatoru; 68-9/960-200; relais-josephine-rangiroa.com. **$$**

An inviting four-poster bed in one of the hotel's guest rooms.

Coral details
in one
of Raimiti's
cottages.

FAKARAVA, FRENCH POLYNESIA

Raimiti

Visitors with castaway fantasies will find plenty of inspiration at Raimiti, a South Seas hideaway on a narrow motu 90 minutes by motorboat from the island of Fakarava. Set in a coconut forest, the 10 palm-thatched cottages are simple and rustic, evoking the sea with driftwood furnishings and accents of coral from the reef offshore. There's no electricity to speak of—only kerosene lanterns and solar-powered lamps to light your way along sandy paths fringed with fragrant *tiare* flowers. During the day, schools of glinting jackfish and graceful manta rays beckon snorkelers to the lagoon. In the evening, swaying coral garlands provide the sound track for dinner in the restaurant, which serves ceviche-like *poisson cru* made with fish from the waters just beyond your table.

144 Rotoava; 68-9/710-763; raimiti.com. **$$$$**

A guest room. Above: Fresh banana bread served at breakfast.

Hotel Overall

SINGITA GRUMETI
Serengeti National Park, Tanzania

THE FLAME TREES OF THIKA
MEMORIES OF AN AFRICAN CHILDHOOD

The Progress Paradox / Gregg Easterbrook

World's Best
Awards

The Top 100 Hotels

1 **Singita Grumeti**
Serengeti National Park, Tanzania 98.25

2 **Triple Creek Ranch** Darby, Montana 98.22

3 **Southern Ocean Lodge**
Kangaroo Island, Australia 97.87

4 **Oberoi Udaivilas** Udaipur, India 97.50

5 **Discovery Shores**
Boracay, Philippines 96.77

6 **Nayara Hotel, Spa & Gardens**
La Fortuna, Costa Rica 96.36

7 **Singita Kruger National Park**
South Africa 96.33

8 **Palacio Duhau – Park Hyatt**
Buenos Aires 96.13

9 **Ngorongoro Sopa Lodge** Tanzania 95.85

10 **Singita Sabi Sand**
Kruger National Park Area, South Africa 95.74

11 **The Peninsula** Bangkok 95.72

12 **Wentworth Mansion**
Charleston, South Carolina 95.47

13 **Sabi Sabi Private Game Reserve Lodges** Kruger National Park Area, South Africa 95.40

14 **One&Only** Cape Town 95.33

15 **Kirawira Luxury Tented Camp** Serengeti National Park, Tanzania 95.27

16 **Lodge at Kauri Cliffs**
Matauri Bay, New Zealand 95.25

17 **Mombo Camp and Little Mombo Camp**
Moremi Game Reserve, Botswana 95.17

18 **Mandarin Oriental** Bangkok 95.04

19 **Tu Tu'tun Lodge** Gold Beach, Oregon 95.00

20 **Fairmont Mara Safari Club**
Masai Mara National Reserve, Kenya 94.84

21 **Osprey at Beaver Creek** Colorado 94.75

22 **Waldorf Astoria (formerly the Elysian Hotel)** Chicago 94.67

23 **The Peninsula** Shanghai 94.63

24 **Four Seasons Hotel Istanbul at the Bosphorus** 94.54

25 **Lizard Island Resort**
Great Barrier Reef, Australia 94.53

26 **Hotel Santa Caterina** Amalfi, Italy 94.48

27 **andBeyond Kichwa Tembo**
Masai Mara National Reserve, Kenya 94.48

28 **Oberoi Rajvilas** Jaipur, India 94.45

29 **Hotel Salto Chico/Explora Patagonia**
Torres del Paine, Chile 94.40

30 **The Sebastian** Vail, Colorado 94.37

31 **The Peninsula** Hong Kong 94.34

32 **The Willcox** Aiken, South Carolina 94.25 Ⓢ

33 **Live Aqua** Cancún, Mexico 94.22

33 **Saxon Boutique Hotel, Villas & Spa**
Johannesburg, South Africa 94.22

35 **Rosewood Mansion on Turtle Creek**
Dallas 94.18

36 **Umaid Bhawan Palace**
Jodhpur, India 94.07

37 **Capella** Singapore 93.85

38 **Grand Velas** Riviera Maya, Mexico 93.80

39 **Amansara** Siem Reap, Cambodia 93.78

40 **Four Seasons Resort Hualalai**
Hawaii, the Big Island 93.75

41 **Twelve Apostles Hotel & Spa**
Cape Town 93.71

42 **Four Seasons Resort**
Bora-Bora, French Polynesia 93.68

43 **The Peninsula** Chicago 93.66

44 **Cape Grace** Cape Town 93.65

45 **Palazzo Avino (formerly Palazzo Sasso)** Ravello, Italy 93.64

46 **Fairmont Mount Kenya Safari Club**
Nanyuki, Kenya 93.60

47 **Oberoi Amarvilas** Agra, India 93.56

48 **Lodge at Doonbeg**
County Clare, Ireland 93.56 Ⓢ

49 **Four Seasons Hotel Gresham Palace**
Budapest 93.50

49 **Huka Lodge** Taupo, New Zealand 93.50

49 **Morrison House**
Alexandria, Virginia 93.50 Ⓢ

KEY Ⓢ *Great Value ($250 or less)*

NO2 **Hotel Overall**
TRIPLE CREEK RANCH
Darby, Montana

Top 100 Hotels (cont.)

world's best awards

245

Continental U.S.

RESORTS (40 ROOMS OR MORE)

1 **Osprey at Beaver Creek** Colorado 94.75
2 **The Sebastian** Vail, Colorado 94.37
3 **Pines Lodge** Beaver Creek, Colorado 93.48
4 **Ocean House**
Watch Hill, Rhode Island 93.14
5 **Blackberry Farm** Walland, Tennessee 92.72
6 **Inn at Palmetto Bluff, an Auberge
Resort** Bluffton, South Carolina 92.65
7 **Amangani** Jackson Hole, Wyoming 92.62
8 **Ritz-Carlton Bachelor Gulch**
Avon, Colorado 92.58
9 **Wequassett Resort & Golf Club**
Chatham, Massachusetts 92.57
10 **Ritz-Carlton, Dove Mountain**
Marana, Arizona 92.38
11 **Sanctuary at Kiawah Island Golf
Resort** South Carolina 92.10
12 **Allison Inn & Spa** Newberg, Oregon 92.03
13 **Stein Eriksen Lodge**
Deer Valley, Utah 91.60
14 **Waldorf Astoria** Park City, Utah 91.43 ⓢ
15 **St. Regis Deer Valley** Park City, Utah 91.20
16 **Royal Palms Resort & Spa** Phoenix 91.15
17 **San Ysidro Ranch**
Santa Barbara, California 90.97
18 **L'Auberge de Sedona** Arizona 90.95
19 **Wentworth by the Sea, a Marriott Hotel &
Spa** New Castle, New Hampshire 90.93
20 **Lodge at Pebble Beach** California 90.91
21 **Ritz-Carlton** Lake Tahoe, California 90.88
22 **The Broadmoor** Colorado Springs 90.83
23 **Four Seasons Resort Scottsdale at
Troon North** Arizona 90.76
24 **Four Seasons Resort & Club Dallas
at Las Colinas** Irving, Texas 90.74
25 **Montage Laguna Beach** California 90.74
26 **Ritz-Carlton** Naples, Florida 90.68
27 **Old Edwards Inn & Spa**
Highlands, North Carolina 90.67
28 **Ritz-Carlton**
Laguna Niguel, California 90.64
29 **Auberge du Soleil**
Rutherford, California 90.58
30 **Park Hyatt Beaver Creek Resort & Spa**
Avon, Colorado 90.58
31 **Williamsburg Inn** Virginia 90.44
32 **White Elephant**
Nantucket, Massachusetts 90.44
33 **Four Seasons Resort** Vail, Colorado 90.43
34 **Four Seasons Resort**
Jackson Hole, Wyoming 90.36
35 **Calistoga Ranch** California 90.33
36 **Little Nell** Aspen, Colorado 90.17
37 **Pinehurst Resort** North Carolina 90.16
38 **Solage Calistoga** California 90.08

39 **Keswick Hall at Monticello**
Virginia 90.00 ⓢ
40 **Bardessono** Yountville, California 89.94
41 **Harbor View Hotel & Resort**
Edgartown, Massachusetts 89.91
42 **Inn at Spanish Bay**
Pebble Beach, California 89.88
43 **Lodge & Club at Ponte Vedra Beach**
Florida 89.85
44 **Inn by the Sea** Cape Elizabeth, Maine 89.74
45 **Pelican Hill** Newport Coast, California 89.74
46 **Montage Deer Valley** Park City, Utah 89.68
47 **The Phoenician, a Luxury Collection
Resort** Scottsdale, Arizona 89.66
48 **The Greenbrier**
White Sulphur Springs, West Virginia 89.65
49 **Enchantment Resort**
Sedona, Arizona 89.55
50 **Ritz-Carlton** Palm Beach, Florida 89.46

**LARGE CITY HOTELS
(100 ROOMS OR MORE)**

1 **Waldorf Astoria (formerly the
Elysian Hotel)** Chicago 94.67
2 **Rosewood Mansion on Turtle Creek**
Dallas 94.18
3 **The Peninsula** Chicago 93.66
4 **Hermitage Hotel** Nashville 92.72
5 **Trump International Hotel & Tower**
New York City 92.40
6 **Four Seasons Hotel** New York City 92.28
7 **St. Regis** Atlanta 92.26
8 **The Peninsula**
Beverly Hills, California 92.23
9 **Beverly Wilshire in Beverly Hills
(A Four Seasons Hotel)** California 92.00
10 **Mandarin Oriental** Las Vegas 91.86
11 **Umstead Hotel & Spa**
Cary, North Carolina 91.36
12 **Mandarin Oriental** Boston 91.17
13 **Four Seasons Hotel Los Angeles at
Beverly Hills** 91.14
13 **Ritz-Carlton New York, Central Park**
91.14
15 **Beverly Hills Hotel & Bungalows**
California 91.07
16 **The Setai** Miami Beach 90.96
17 **Hotel Bel-Air** Los Angeles 90.71
18 **Andaz (formerly the Avia)**
Savannah, Georgia 90.67 ⓢ
19 **The Peninsula** New York City 90.47
20 **Four Seasons Hotel** Boston 90.45
21 **Mandarin Oriental (formerly the
Mansion on Peachtree)** Atlanta 90.35
22 **Four Seasons Hotel** Chicago 90.33
23 **Boston Harbor Hotel at Rowes Wharf**
90.30

24 **Montage Beverly Hills** California 90.24
25 **Four Seasons Hotel** Las Vegas 90.17 ⓢ
26 **Rittenhouse Hotel** Philadelphia 90.07
27 **Park Hyatt** Chicago 90.04
28 **Roosevelt New Orleans,
a Waldorf Astoria Hotel** 90.04 ⓢ
29 **Trump International Hotel & Tower**
Chicago 90.00
30 **Four Seasons Hotel** Atlanta 89.76 ⓢ
31 **Four Seasons Hotel** Denver 89.74
32 **Hotel 1000** Seattle 89.60
33 **Charleston Place** South Carolina 89.59 ⓢ
34 **Grand Bohemian Hotel**
Asheville, North Carolina 89.57 ⓢ
35 **Ritz-Carlton** New Orleans 89.57 ⓢ
36 **Ritz-Carlton Boston Common** 89.55
37 **Ritz-Carlton Chicago
(A Four Seasons Hotel)** 89.42
38 **Cosmopolitan of Las Vegas** 89.38 ⓢ
39 **Ritz-Carlton** Philadelphia 89.38
40 **Mandarin Oriental** New York City 89.27
41 **Proximity Hotel**
Greensboro, North Carolina 89.25
42 **Ritz-Carlton, Pentagon City**
Arlington, Virginia 89.17
43 **St. Regis** San Francisco 89.15
44 **Hotel Commonwealth** Boston 89.09
44 **The Pierre** New York City 89.09
46 **Heathman Hotel** Portland, Oregon 89.04
47 **Mandarin Oriental** Miami 89.04
48 **Windsor Court Hotel**
New Orleans 89.03 ⓢ
49 **Hotel Palomar** Philadelphia 89.00 ⓢ
50 **Ritz-Carlton**
Charlotte, North Carolina 88.97

**SMALL CITY HOTELS
(FEWER THAN 100 ROOMS)**

1 **Wentworth Mansion**
Charleston, South Carolina 95.47
2 **Morrison House** Alexandria,
Virginia 93.50 ⓢ
3 **XV Beacon** Boston 92.35
4 **Market Pavilion Hotel**
Charleston, South Carolina 91.79 ⓢ
5 **Rosewood Inn of the Anasazi**
Santa Fe, New Mexico 90.22
6 **21c Museum Hotel**
Louisville, Kentucky 89.39 ⓢ
7 **Planters Inn**
Charleston, South Carolina 88.84 ⓢ
8 **Inn at the Market** Seattle 88.76
9 **Delamar Greenwich Harbor**
Greenwich, Connecticut 88.47
10 **Ritz-Carlton Georgetown**
Washington, D.C. 87.91

246

Continental U.S. (cont.)

Canada

INNS AND SMALL LODGES
(FEWER THAN 40 ROOMS)

1   **Triple Creek Ranch** Darby, Montana 98.22
2   **Tu Tu'tun Lodge** Gold Beach, Oregon 95.00
3   **The Willcox** Aiken, South Carolina 94.25 ⓢ
4   **Amangiri** Canyon Point, Utah 93.33
5   **Post Ranch Inn** Big Sur, California 92.49
6   **Marquesa Hotel** Key West, Florida 91.60
7   **Inn at Little Washington**
    Washington, Virginia 90.94
8   **Mayflower Inn & Spa**
    Washington, Connecticut 90.44
9   **Elizabeth Pointe Lodge**
    Amelia Island, Florida 89.68 ⓢ
10 **Little Palm Island Resort & Spa**
    Torch Key, Florida 89.38

TOP 5 HOTEL SPAS

1   **Allison Inn & Spa**
    Newberg, Oregon 96.05 ⓢ
2   **St. Regis Aspen Resort** Colorado 95.77
3   **Four Seasons Hotel** Las Vegas 95.59
4   **Bardessono Hotel & Spa**
    Yountville, California 95.00
5   **Terranea**
    Rancho Palos Verdes, California 94.62

CITY HOTELS

1   **Auberge Saint-Antoine**
    Quebec City 93.12
2   **Ritz-Carlton** Toronto 89.58
3   **Shangri-La Hotel** Vancouver 88.67
4   **Fairmont Le Château Frontenac**
    Quebec City 87.39
5   **Hotel Grand Pacific**
    Victoria, British Columbia 87.00 ⓢ
6   **Four Seasons Hotel** Vancouver 86.88
7   **Fairmont Empress**
    Victoria, British Columbia 86.81 ⓢ
8   **Loews Hotel Vogue** Montreal 86.50 ⓢ
9   **Wedgewood Hotel & Spa**
    Vancouver 86.10
10 **Fairmont Hotel Vancouver** 86.02

RESORTS

1   **Wickaninnish Inn**
    Tofino, British Columbia 91.33
2   **Sooke Harbour House**
    British Columbia 90.80 ⓢ
3   **Four Seasons Resort**
    Whistler, British Columbia 90.24
4   **Post Hotel & Spa**
    Lake Louise, Alberta 89.93

5   **Fairmont Chateau Whistler**
    British Columbia 88.73
6   **Fairmont Chateau Lake Louise**
    Alberta 88.63
7   **Rimrock Resort Hotel**
    Banff, Alberta 88.15 ⓢ
8   **Fairmont Le Manoir Richelieu**
    La Malbaie, Quebec 88.00 ⓢ
9   **Hilton Whistler Resort & Spa**
    British Columbia 87.06
10 **Westin Whistler Resort & Spa**
    British Columbia 86.89

TOP HOTEL SPA

1   **Fairmont Chateau Whistler**
    British Columbia 93.42

NO 4 Continental U.S. Inn
AMANGIRI *Canyon Point, Utah*

Hawaii

RESORTS

1. **Four Seasons Resort Hualalai**
   Hawaii, the Big Island 93.75
2. **Koa Kea Hotel & Resort** Kauai 92.44
3. **Four Seasons Resort Lanai,
   The Lodge at Koele** 92.32
4. **Four Seasons Resort Maui at Wailea**
   92.19
5. **Halekulani** Oahu 91.05
6. **Kahala Hotel & Resort** Oahu 90.74
7. **Grand Hyatt Kauai Resort & Spa** 89.88
8. **St. Regis Princeville Resort** Kauai 89.43
9. **Royal Hawaiian, a Luxury Collection
   Resort** Oahu 89.42
10. **Mauna Lani Bay Hotel & Bungalows**
    Hawaii, the Big Island 89.05
11. **Fairmont Kea Lani** Maui 88.88
12. **Ritz-Carlton Kapalua** Maui 88.49
13. **Hapuna Beach Prince Hotel**
    Hawaii, the Big Island 88.13
14. **Mauna Kea Beach Hotel**
    Hawaii, the Big Island 87.58
15. **JW Marriott Ihilani Resort & Spa**
    Oahu 86.11
16. **Grand Wailea** Maui 85.72
17. **Fairmont Orchid**
    Hawaii, the Big Island 85.57
18. **Outrigger Reef on the Beach** Oahu 85.44
19. **Four Seasons Resort Lanai at Manele
    Bay** 85.28
20. **Hyatt Regency Waikiki Beach Resort &
    Spa** Oahu 85.26 ⑤
21. **Embassy Suites Waikiki Beach Walk**
    Oahu 84.25
22. **Wailea Beach Marriott Resort & Spa**
    Maui 84.20
23. **Hyatt Regency Maui Resort & Spa** 84.05
24. **Moana Surfrider, a Westin Resort &
    Spa** Oahu 83.36
25. **Hilton Waikoloa Village**
    Hawaii, the Big Island 82.80 ⑤

TOP 3 HOTEL SPAS

1. **Grand Wailea** Maui 94.05
2. **Four Seasons Resort Hualalai**
   Hawaii, the Big Island 94.00
3. **Four Seasons Resort Maui at Wailea**
   91.46

№5 **Hawaii Resort**
HALEKULANI *Oahu*

NO.1 Caribbean Resort
THE REEFS
Southampton, Bermuda

The Caribbean, Bermuda + The Bahamas

RESORTS

1 **The Reefs** Bermuda 92.71
2 **Nisbet Plantation Beach Club**
   Nevis 92.00
3 **Eden Rock** St. Bart's 91.86
4 **Jade Mountain** St. Lucia 91.52
5 **Couples Sans Souci**
   St. Ann, Jamaica 90.84
6 **Couples Tower Isle**
   St. Mary, Jamaica 90.71
7 **Biras Creek Resort**
   Virgin Gorda, British Virgin Islands 90.44
8 **Couples Negril** Jamaica 90.36
9 **Couples Swept Away**
   Negril, Jamaica 90.29
10 **Hotel Saint-Barth Isle de France**
   St. Bart's 90.22
11 **Ritz-Carlton**
   Grand Cayman, Cayman Islands 89.18
12 **Regent Palms** Turks and Caicos 88.95

13 **Rosewood Tucker's Point** Bermuda 88.42
14 **Ocean Club** Turks and Caicos 88.27
15 **Four Seasons Resort** Nevis 88.14
16 **W Retreat & Spa**
   Vieques, Puerto Rico 87.85
17 **Ritz-Carlton** St. Thomas,
   U.S. Virgin Islands 87.71
18 **Rock House Hotel**
   Harbour Island, Bahamas 87.24
19 **Anse Chastanet Resort** St. Lucia 87.20
19 **Ladera Resort** St. Lucia 87.20
21 **Caneel Bay, A Rosewood Resort**
   St. John, U.S. Virgin Islands 87.13
22 **Rosewood Little Dix Bay**
   Virgin Gorda, British Virgin Islands 87.07
23 **Secrets Wild Orchid**
   Montego Bay, Jamaica 87.06
24 **Las Casitas Village, a Waldorf Astoria**
   Resort Fajardo, Puerto Rico 86.82
25 **Sandy Lane** Barbados 86.55

TOP 3 HOTEL SPAS

1 **Sandy Lane** Barbados 93.85
2 **Couples Sans Souci**
   St. Mary, Jamaica 93.07
3 **The Reefs** Southampton,
   Bermuda 92.60

Mexico

RESORTS

1 **Live Aqua** Cancún 94.22
2 **Grand Velas** Riviera Maya 93.80
3 **Capella Pedregal** Los Cabos 93.29
4 **La Casa Que Canta** Zihuatanejo 93.20
5 **St. Regis Punta Mita Resort** 91.72
6 **One&Only Palmilla** Los Cabos 91.14
7 **Las Ventanas al Paraíso, A Rosewood**
   Resort Los Cabos 91.09
8 **Four Seasons Resort** Punta Mita 90.52
9 **Secrets Maroma Beach**
   Riviera Cancún 90.47
10 **Fairmont Acapulco Princess** 89.76 ⓢ
11 **Banyan Tree Mayakoba Resort & Spa**
   Riviera Maya 89.43
12 **Ritz-Carlton** Cancún 89.18
13 **Grand Velas Riviera Nayarit**
   Nuevo Vallarta 88.96
14 **Esperanza, an Auberge Resort**
   Los Cabos 88.90
15 **Royal Hideaway Playacar**
   Riviera Maya 88.71
16 **Iberostar Paraíso Maya**
   Riviera Maya 88.50 ⓢ
17 **Fairmont Mayakoba** Riviera Maya 88.00
18 **Secrets Marquis** Los Cabos 87.78
19 **Pueblo Bonito Pacifica Resort & Spa**
   Los Cabos 87.61
20 **Pueblo Bonito Sunset Beach Resort &**
   Spa Los Cabos 87.03 ⓢ

CITY HOTELS

1 **Four Seasons Hotel México, D.F.**
   Mexico City 90.40
2 **JW Marriott Hotel** Mexico City 86.48
3 **Camino Real Polanco** Mexico City 84.00 ⓢ

TOP 3 HOTEL SPAS

1 **Capella Pedregal** Los Cabos 97.65
2 **Grand Velas Riviera Maya**
   Playa del Carmen 97.50
3 **Esperanza, an Auberge Resort**
   Los Cabos 94.85

Mexico Resort
ONE&ONLY PALMILLA
Los Cabos

Central+South America

RESORTS

1 **Nayara Hotel, Spa & Gardens**
La Fortuna, Costa Rica 96.36

2 **Hotel Salto Chico/Explora Patagonia**
Torres del Paine, Chile 94.40

3 **Llao Llao Hotel & Resort, Golf-Spa**
Bariloche, Argentina 92.31

4 **Four Seasons Resort Costa Rica
at Peninsula Papagayo** 91.83

5 **Inkaterra Machu Picchu Pueblo Hotel**
Peru 91.63

6 **Los Sueños Marriott Ocean & Golf
Resort** Playa Herradura, Costa Rica 88.67

7 **Lodge at Chaa Creek**
San Ignacio, Belize 88.24

8 **Hotel Arenal Kioro**
La Fortuna, Costa Rica 86.67

9 **Machu Picchu Sanctuary Lodge**
Peru 84.70

10 **Westin Golf Resort & Spa, Playa
Conchal—An All-Inclusive Resort**
Costa Rica 84.48 Ⓢ

CITY HOTELS

Palacio Duhau - Park Hyatt
Buenos Aires 96.13

Hotel Museo Casa Santo Domingo
Antigua, Guatemala 92.67 Ⓢ

Grand Hyatt Santiago, Chile 92.62

Hotel Monasterio Cuzco, Peru 90.15

InterContinental Buenos Aires 90.11 Ⓢ

JW Marriott Hotel Lima, Peru 90.07

Alvear Palace Hotel Buenos Aires 90.05

Four Seasons Hotel Buenos Aires 89.29

Park Hyatt Mendoza, Argentina 89.19

Ritz-Carlton Santiago, Chile 89.04

Faena Hotel & Universe
Buenos Aires 87.47

12 **W Santiago** Chile 87.00

13 **Miraflores Park Hotel** Lima, Peru 85.42

14 **Park Tower, Buenos Aires,
a Luxury Collection Hotel** 85.26

15 **Hilton** Buenos Aires 84.70

TOP 5 HOTEL SPAS

1 **Nayara Hotel, Spa & Gardens**
La Fortuna, Costa Rica 95.39 Ⓢ

2 **Four Seasons Resort Costa Rica at
Peninsula Papagayo** 91.20

3 **Tabacón Grand Spa Thermal Resort**
La Fortuna, Costa Rica 87.35

4 **Los Sueños Marriott Ocean & Golf
Resort** Herradura Bay, Costa Rica 84.09

5 **Inkaterra Machu Picchu Pueblo Hotel**
Peru 83.00 Ⓢ

NO.1 **Central+South America
City Hotel**
PALACIO DUHAU - PARK HYATT
Buenos Aires

Europe

RESORTS (40 ROOMS OR MORE)

1. **Hotel Santa Caterina** Amalfi, Italy 94.48
2. **Palazzo Avino (formerly Palazzo Sasso)** Ravello, Italy **93.64**
3. **Lodge at Doonbeg** County Clare, Ireland 93.56 Ⓢ
4. **Sheen Falls Lodge** County Kerry, Ireland 93.40
5. **Le Sirenuse** Positano, Italy 93.33
6. **Hotel Caruso** Ravello, Italy 93.25
7. **Villa d'Este** Cernobbio, Italy 91.61
8. **Dromoland Castle** County Clare, Ireland 91.48
9. **Il San Pietro di Positano** Italy 91.47
10. **Hotel Splendido** Portofino, Italy 91.37

LARGE CITY HOTELS (100 ROOMS OR MORE)

1. **Four Seasons Hotel Istanbul at the Bosphorus** 94.54
2. **Four Seasons Hotel Gresham Palace** Budapest 93.50
3. **Hôtel Plaza Athénée** Paris 92.86
4. **Hotel Bristol, a Luxury Collection Hotel** Vienna 92.46
5. **Four Seasons Hotel Ritz** Lisbon 92.12
6. **Four Seasons Hotel Milano** Milan 92.00
7. **Hôtel Hermitage** Monte Carlo, Monaco 91.75
8. **Four Seasons Hotel, Firenze** Florence 91.75
9. **Four Seasons Hotel London at Park Lane** 91.68
10. **Four Seasons Hotel George V** Paris 91.58
11. **Ritz-Carlton** Moscow 91.56
12. **Le Méridien Bristol** Warsaw 91.53 Ⓢ
13. **Merrion Hotel** Dublin 91.50
14. **Stafford London by Kempinski** 91.47
15. **Hôtel de Paris** Monte Carlo, Monaco 91.36

SMALL CITY HOTELS (FEWER THAN 100 ROOMS)

1. **Four Seasons Hotel Istanbul at Sultanahmet** 93.36
2. **Milestone Hotel** London 92.83
3. **The Lanesborough** London 90.82
4. **Ca' Sagredo** Venice 90.60
5. **Soho Hotel** London 90.59
6. **Mandarin Oriental** Munich 90.00
7. **Hotel Goldener Hirsch Salzburg, a Luxury Collection Hotel** Austria 89.71
8. **Hotel Hassler Roma** Rome 89.33
9. **La Mirande** Avignon, France 88.21
10. **41** London 88.14

INNS AND SMALL COUNTRY HOTELS (FEWER THAN 40 ROOMS)

1. **Katikies Hotel** Santorini, Greece 93.07
2. **Hôtel Crillon le Brave** Provence, France 93.05
3. **Domaine des Hauts de Loire** Onzain, France 93.00 Ⓢ
4. **Domaine Les Crayères** Reims, France 92.38
5. **L'Oustau de Baumanière** Les Baux-de-Provence, France 91.78
6. **Hôtel Château Eza** Èze Village, France 89.33
7. **Cliveden House** Taplow, England 89.33
8. **Villa Gallici** Aix-en-Provence, France 88.32
9. **La Chèvre d'Or** Èze Village, France 87.43
10. **Il Falconiere** Cortona, Italy 85.91

TOP 5 HOTEL SPAS

1. **Ritz Paris** (closed until 2014) 94.09
2. **Four Seasons Hotel, Firenze** Florence 93.21
3. **Four Seasons Hotel George V** Paris 92.19
4. **Rome Cavalieri, Waldorf Astoria Hotels & Resorts** 91.25
5. **Le Sirenuse** Positano, Italy 90.77

Europe Resort
HOTEL SANTA CATERINA
Amalfi, Italy

Africa+The Middle East

LODGES AND RESORTS

1. **Singita Grumeti**
Serengeti National Park, Tanzania 98.25
2. **Singita Kruger National Park**
South Africa 96.33
3. **Ngorongoro Sopa Lodge** Tanzania 95.85
4. **Singita Sabi Sand**
Kruger National Park Area, South Africa 95.74
5. **Sabi Sabi Private Game Reserve Lodges**
Kruger National Park, South Africa 95.40
6. **Kirawira Luxury Tented Camp**
Serengeti National Park, Tanzania 95.27
7. **Mombo Camp and Little Mombo Camp**
Moremi Game Reserve, Botswana 95.17
8. **Fairmont Mara Safari Club**
Masai Mara National Reserve, Kenya 94.84
9. **andBeyond Kichwa Tembo**
Masai Mara National Reserve, Kenya 94.48
10. **Fairmont Mount Kenya Safari Club**
Nanyuki, Kenya 93.60
11. **Serengeti Sopa Lodge**
Serengeti National Park, Tanzania 92.89
12. **andBeyond Ngorongoro Crater Lodge**
Tanzania 92.88

13. **Tortilis Camp**
Amboseli National Park, Kenya 92.40
14. **Giraffe Manor** Nairobi, Kenya 91.53
15. **Royal Livingstone**
Victoria Falls, Zambia 89.90
16. **Le Quartier Français**
Franschhoek, South Africa 89.42
17. **MalaMala Game Reserve**
Kruger National Park Area, South Africa 89.27
18. **Amboseli Serena Safari Lodge**
Amboseli National Park, Kenya 88.83
19. **Mara Serena Safari Lodge**
Masai Mara National Reserve, Kenya 88.00
20. **Kempinski Hotel Ishtar**
Dead Sea, Jordan 87.60

CITY HOTELS

1. **One&Only** Cape Town 95.33
2. **Saxon Boutique Hotel, Villas & Spa**
Johannesburg, South Africa 94.22
3. **Twelve Apostles Hotel & Spa**
Cape Town 93.71
4. **Cape Grace** Cape Town 93.65
5. **Four Seasons Hotel Cairo at the First Residence** 91.64

6. **Mena House Oberoi** Cairo 91.27 $
7. **La Mamounia** Marrakesh, Morocco 90.52
8. **Four Seasons Hotel Cairo at Nile Plaza** 90.49 $
9. **Mount Nelson Hotel** Cape Town 90.20
10. **Burj Al Arab** Dubai 89.82
11. **The Westcliff**
Johannesburg, South Africa 89.55
12. **Fairmont The Norfolk**
Nairobi, Kenya 89.06
13. **Victoria & Alfred Hotel** Cape Town 88.16
14. **King David Hotel** Jerusalem 88.00
15. **Sofitel Winter Palace** Luxor, Egypt 87.20 $

TOP HOTEL SPA

Twelve Apostles Hotel & Spa
Cape Town 92.50 $

N02 **Africa Resort**
SINGITA KRUGER NATIONAL PARK
South Africa

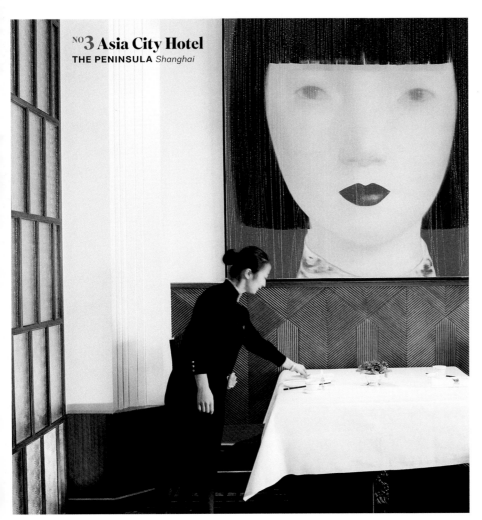

NO 3 Asia City Hotel
THE PENINSULA *Shanghai*

26 **La Résidence d'Angkor**
    Siem Reap, Cambodia 90.10
27 **The Oberoi** Mumbai 90.00 ⓢ
28 **The Peninsula** Tokyo 89.91
29 **Fullerton Hotel** Singapore 89.74
30 **Mandarin Oriental** Singapore 89.53

TOP 5 HOTEL SPAS
1 **Discovery Shores**
   Boracay, Philippines 97.50 ⓢ
2 **Four Seasons Resort Bali at Jimbaran
   Bay** Indonesia 97.00
3 **Mandarin Oriental** Bangkok 95.71
4 **Sofitel Angkor Phokeethra Golf & Spa
   Resort** Siem Reap, Cambodia 95.65 ⓢ
5 **Capella** Singapore 95.29

Australia, New Zealand + The South Pacific

RESORTS
1 **Southern Ocean Lodge**
   Kangaroo Island, Australia 97.87
2 **Lodge at Kauri Cliffs**
   Matauri Bay, New Zealand 95.25
3 **Lizard Island Resort**
   Great Barrier Reef, Australia 94.53
4 **Four Seasons Resort**
   Bora-Bora, French Polynesia 93.68
5 **Huka Lodge** Taupo, New Zealand 93.50
6 **St. Regis** Bora-Bora, French Polynesia 91.25
7 **Hayman** Great Barrier Reef, Australia 89.00
8 **Hilton Bora Bora Nui Resort & Spa**
   French Polynesia 85.47
9 **Hilton Moorea Lagoon Resort & Spa**
   French Polynesia 84.63
10 **Sheraton Mirage**
   Port Douglas, Australia 80.27 ⓢ

CITY HOTELS
1 **The Langham** Melbourne 90.55
2 **Shangri-La Hotel** Sydney 88.83
3 **Park Hyatt** Sydney 88.20
4 **The George** Christchurch, New Zealand 87.77
5 **Observatory Hotel** Sydney 86.82
6 **Sofitel Queenstown Hotel & Spa**
   New Zealand 86.67
7 **Sydney Harbour Marriott at
   Circular Quay** 86.51
8 **Four Seasons Hotel** Sydney 85.36
9 **Park Hyatt** Melbourne 85.28
10 **Grand Hyatt** Melbourne 85.00

TOP HOTEL SPA
1 **Four Seasons Resort**
   Bora-Bora, French Polynesia 91.82

Asia

RESORTS
1 **Oberoi Udaivilas** Udaipur, India 97.50
2 **Discovery Shores** Boracay, Philippines 96.77
3 **Oberoi Rajvilas** Jaipur, India 94.45
4 **Umaid Bhawan Palace** Jodhpur, India 94.07
5 **Capella** Singapore 93.85
6 **Amansara** Siem Reap, Cambodia 93.78
7 **Oberoi Amarvilas** Agra, India 93.56
8 **Rambagh Palace** Jaipur, India 93.00
9 **Taj Lake Palace** Udaipur, India 92.92
10 **Sofitel Angkor Phokeethra Golf & Spa
   Resort** Siem Reap, Cambodia 92.86 ⓢ
11 **La Résidence Phou Vao**
   Luang Prabang, Laos 92.80
12 **Four Seasons Resort**
   Chiang Mai, Thailand 92.68
13 **Mandarin Oriental Dhara Dhevi**
   Chiang Mai, Thailand 92.38
14 **Four Seasons Resort Bali at Jimbaran
   Bay** Indonesia 89.47
15 **Ayana Resort & Spa** Bali, Indonesia 88.80

CITY HOTELS
1 **The Peninsula** Bangkok 95.72
2 **Mandarin Oriental** Bangkok 95.04

3 **The Peninsula** Shanghai 94.63
4 **The Peninsula** Hong Kong 94.34
5 **Ritz-Carlton Millenia** Singapore 92.75
6 **Park Hyatt Saigon**
   Ho Chi Minh City, Vietnam 92.62
7 **Taj Mahal Hotel** New Delhi 92.00
8 **Sofitel Legend Metropole**
   Hanoi, Vietnam 91.84 ⓢ
9 **Mandarin Oriental** Hong Kong 91.66
10 **The Peninsula** Beijing 91.64
11 **Taj Mahal Palace** Mumbai 91.53
12 **Raffles Hotel** Singapore 91.42
13 **Ritz-Carlton, Financial Street**
   Beijing 91.25
14 **Ritz-Carlton**
   Kuala Lumpur, Malaysia 91.20 ⓢ
15 **Park Hyatt** Tokyo 91.16
16 **The Shilla** Seoul 91.16
17 **Shangri-La Hotel** Singapore 91.14 ⓢ
18 **Four Seasons Hotel** Hong Kong 91.12
19 **Royal Orchid Sheraton Hotel & Towers**
   Bangkok 90.78
20 **Grand Hyatt Erawan** Bangkok 90.46 ⓢ
21 **Shangri-La Hotel** Bangkok 90.42 ⓢ
22 **Pudong Shangri-La** Shanghai 90.40
23 **Grand Hyatt** Tokyo 90.35
24 **The Sukhothai** Bangkok 90.35
25 **Leela Palace**
   Bengaluru (Bangalore), India 90.11

Hotel Salto Chico/
Explora Patagonia, in
Chile's Torres del
Paine National Park.

T+L 500

United States

ALABAMA
Point Clear
ⓢ **Grand Hotel Marriott Resort, Golf Club & Spa** 87.64 800/228-9290; marriott.com. **$$**

ARIZONA
Phoenix/Scottsdale
Four Seasons Resort Scottsdale at Troon North 90.76 10600 E. Crescent Moon Dr., Scottsdale; 800/332-3442; fourseasons.com. **$$$**

JW Marriott Camelback Inn Resort & Spa 87.58 5402 E. Lincoln Dr., Scottsdale; 800/228-9290; jwmarriott.com. **$$$**

The Phoenician, a Luxury Collection Resort 89.66 6000 E. Camelback Rd., Scottsdale; 800/325-3589; thephoenician.com. **$$$**

Royal Palms Resort & Spa 91.15 5200 E. Camelback Rd., Phoenix; 800/672-6011; royalpalmshotel.com. **$$$**

Sanctuary on Camelback Mountain Resort & Spa 89.10 5700 E. McDonald Dr., Paradise Valley; 800/245-2051; sanctuaryoncamelback.com. **$$$**

Sedona
Enchantment Resort 89.55 800/826-4180; enchantmentresort.com. **$$**

L'Auberge de Sedona 90.95 800/272-6777; lauberge.com. **$$**

Tucson
ⓢ **Ritz-Carlton, Dove Mountain** 92.38 15000 N. Secret Springs Dr.; 800/241-3333; ritzcarlton.com. **$$**

CALIFORNIA
Big Sur
Post Ranch Inn 92.49 888/524-4787; postranchinn.com. **$$$$**

Half Moon Bay
Ritz-Carlton 89.10 800/241-3333; ritzcarlton.com. **$$$**

Lake Tahoe
Ritz-Carlton 90.88 Truckee; 800/241-3333; ritzcarlton.com. **$$$**

Los Angeles Area
Beverly Hills Hotel, Dorchester Collection 91.07 9641 Sunset Blvd., Beverly Hills; 800/650-1842; beverlyhillshotel.com. **$$$$**

Beverly Wilshire, a Four Seasons Hotel 92.00 9500 Wilshire Blvd., Beverly Hills; 800/332-3442; fourseasons.com. **$$$$**

Four Seasons Hotel Los Angeles at Beverly Hills 91.14 300 S. Doheny Dr., Los Angeles; 800/332-3442; fourseasons.com. **$$$**

Hotel Bel-Air, Dorchester Collection 90.71 701 Stone Canyon Rd., Los Angeles; 800/650-1842; hotelbelair.com. **$$$$**

L'Ermitage Beverly Hills 88.69 9291 Burton Way, Beverly Hills; 877/235-7582; lermitagebh.com. **$$$**

Montage Beverly Hills 90.24 225 N. Canon Dr., Beverly Hills; 888/860-0788; montagebeverlyhills.com. **$$$**

Peninsula Beverly Hills 92.23 9882 S. Santa Monica Blvd., Beverly Hills; 866/382-8388; peninsula.com. **$$$$**

Shutters on the Beach 88.64 1 Pico Blvd., Santa Monica; 800/334-9000; shuttersonthebeach.com. **$$$$**

Terranea 89.02 100 Terranea Way, Rancho Palos Verdes; 866/802-8000; terranea.com. **$$$**

Napa/Sonoma
Auberge du Soleil 90.58 Rutherford; 800/348-5406; aubergedusoleil.com. **$$$$**

Bardessono Hotel, Restaurant & Spa 89.94 Yountville; 877/932-5333; bardessono.com. **$$$$**

Calistoga Ranch, an Auberge Resort 90.33 Calistoga; 800/942-4220; calistogaranch.com. **$$$$**

Carneros Inn 88.20 Napa; 888/400-9000; thecarnerosinn.com. **$$$$**

Meadowood Napa Valley 88.62 St. Helena; 800/458-8080; meadowood.com. **$$$$**

Solage Calistoga 90.08 Calistoga; 866/942-7442; solagecalistoga.com. **$$$$**

Villagio Inn & Spa 89.03 Yountville; 800/351-1133; villagio.com. **$$$**

Orange County
Montage Laguna Beach 90.74 Laguna Beach; 866/271-6951; montagelagunabeach.com. **$$$$**

Resort at Pelican Hill 89.74 Newport Beach; 800/820-6800; pelicanhill.com. **$$$**

Ritz-Carlton, Laguna Niguel 90.64 Dana Point; 800/241-3333; ritzcarlton.com. **$$$**

St. Regis Monarch Beach 88.88 Dana Point; 877/787-3447; stregis.com. **$$$**

Pebble Beach
Inn at Spanish Bay 89.88 800/654-9300; pebblebeach.com. **$$$$**

Lodge at Pebble Beach 90.91 800/654-9300; pebblebeach.com. **$$$$**

San Francisco Area
Cavallo Point— the Lodge at the Golden Gate 89.39 Sausalito; 888/651-2003; cavallopoint.com. **$$**

Ritz-Carlton 88.52 600 Stockton St.; 800/241-3333; ritzcarlton.com. **$$$**

St. Regis 89.15 125 3rd St.; 877/787-3447; stregis.com. **$$$**

Taj Campton Place 88.27 340 Stockton St.; 866/969-1825; tajhotels.com. **$$$$**

Santa Barbara Area
Four Seasons Resort The Biltmore 88.57 Montecito; 800/332-3442; fourseasons.com. **$$$$**

San Ysidro Ranch 90.97 Montecito; 888/767-3966; sanysidroranch.com. **$$$$**

COLORADO
Aspen
Little Nell 90.17 888/843-6355; thelittlenell.com. **$$$$**

Beaver Creek
Osprey at Beaver Creek, a RockResort 94.75 866/621-7625; rockresorts.com. **$$$$**

Park Hyatt Beaver Creek Resort & Spa 90.58 877/875-4658; park.hyatt.com. **$$$$**

Pines Lodge, a RockResort 93.48 866/605-7625; rockresorts.com. **$$$$**

Ritz-Carlton, Bachelor Gulch 92.58 800/241-3333; ritzcarlton.com. **$$$$**

Colorado Springs
The Broadmoor 90.83 866/837-9520; broadmoor.com. **$$$**

Denver
Four Seasons Hotel 89.74 1111 14th St.; 800/332-3442; fourseasons.com. **$$**

Telluride
Hotel Madeline (formerly Capella) 88.44 866/475-4403; hotelmadelinetelluride.com. **$$**

Vail
Arrabelle at Vail Square, a RockResort 88.94 866/662-7625; rockresorts.com. **$$$$**

Four Seasons Resort 90.43 800/332-3442; fourseasons.com. **$$$$**

Lodge at Vail, a RockResort 88.44 877/528-7625; rockresorts.com. **$$$$**

The Sebastian 94.37 800/354-6908; thesebastianvail.com. **$$$$**

The Sonnenalp 89.19 866/284-4411; sonnenalp.com. **$$$$**

CONNECTICUT
Greenwich
Delamar Greenwich Harbor 88.47 866/335-2627; delamargreenwich.com. **$$**

Washington
Mayflower Inn & Spa 90.44 860/868-9466; mayflowerinn.com. **$$$$**

DISTRICT OF COLUMBIA
Washington, D.C.
Four Seasons Hotel 87.56 2800 Pennsylvania Ave. NW; 800/332-3442; fourseasons.com. **$$$**

The Hay-Adams 88.92 800 16th St. NW; 800/853-6807; hayadams.com. **$$$**

Ritz-Carlton Georgetown 87.91 3100 South St. NW; 800/241-3333; ritzcarlton.com. **$$$$**

ⓢ **Sofitel Washington D.C. Lafayette Square** 87.91 806 15th St. NW; 800/763-4835; sofitel.com. **$$**

St. Regis 88.36 923 16th St. NW; 877/787-3447; stregis.com. **$$$$$**

ⓢ **Willard InterContinental** 87.62 1401 Pennsylvania Ave. NW; 800/327-0200; intercontinental.com. **$$**

FLORIDA
Amelia Island
ⓢ **Elizabeth Pointe Lodge** 89.68 800/772-3359; elizabethpointelodge.com. **$$**

KEY **$** *Less than $200*   **$$** *$200 to $350*   **$$$** *$350 to $500*   **$$$$** *$500 to $1,000*   **$$$$$** *More than $1,000*   ⓢ *Great Value ($250 or less)*

The lobby lounge at Koa Kea Hotel & Resort, on Kauai, Hawaii.

Ritz-Carlton 89.15 800/241-3333; ritzcarlton.com. **$$**

Clearwater Beach
Sandpearl Resort 88.29 877/726-3111; sandpearl.com. **$$$**

Florida Keys
Little Palm Island Resort & Spa 89.38 Little Torch Key; 800/343-8567; littlepalmisland.com. **$$$$$**

Marquesa Hotel 91.60 Key West; 800/869-4631; marquesa.com. **$$**

Fort Lauderdale
Ritz-Carlton 87.84 866/241-3333; ritzcarlton.com. **$$$$**

Jacksonville Area
ⓢ **Casa Monica Hotel** 88.36 St. Augustine; 800/213-8903; casamonica.com. **$$**

Lodge & Club at Ponte Vedra Beach 89.85 Ponte Vedra Beach; 800/243-4304; pontevedra.com. **$$**

ⓢ **Ponte Vedra Inn & Club** 87.54 Ponte Vedra Beach; 800/234-7842; pontevedra.com. **$$**

Miami Area
JW Marriott Marquis 87.70 255 Biscayne Blvd. Way, Miami; 800/228-9290; marriott.com. **$$$**

Mandarin Oriental 89.04 500 Brickell Key Dr., Miami; 800/526-6566; mandarinoriental.com. **$$$$**

The Setai 90.96 2001 Collins Ave., Miami Beach; 888/625-7500; setai.com. **$$$$**

Naples
Naples Bay Resort & Spa 87.58 866/605-1199; naplesbayresort.com. **$$**

Ritz-Carlton 90.68 800/241-3333; ritzcarlton.com. **$$$$**

Orlando
Disney's Yacht Club Resort 88.88 407/939-6244; disneyworld.disney.go.com. **$$$**

Ritz-Carlton Orlando, Grande Lakes 89.19 800/241-3333; ritzcarlton.com. **$$$**

ⓢ **Waldorf Astoria** 87.88 800/925-3673; waldorfastoria.com. **$$**

Palm Beach
Brazilian Court Hotel & Beach Club 88.41 800/552-0335; thebrazilian court.com. **$$$**

The Breakers 89.28 888/273-2537; thebreakers.com. **$$$$**

Ritz-Carlton 89.46 800/241-3333; ritzcarlton.com. **$$$$**

Vero Beach
ⓢ **Costa d'Este Beach Resort** 88.63 877/562-9919; costadeste.com. **$$**

GEORGIA
Atlanta
Four Seasons Hotel 89.76 75 14th St.; 800/332-3442; fourseasons.com. **$$$**

ⓢ **InterContinental Buckhead** 88.63 3315 Peachtree Rd. N.E.; 800/327-0200; ichotelsgroup.com. **$$**

Mandarin Oriental (formerly the Mansion on Peachtree) 90.35 3376 Peachtree Rd. N.E.; 800/526-6566; mandarinoriental.com. **$$$**

Ritz-Carlton 88.75 181 Peachtree St.; 800/241-3333; ritzcarlton.com. **$$**

Ritz-Carlton, Buckhead 88.89 3434 Peachtree Rd. N.E.; 800/241-3333; ritzcarlton.com. **$$$**

St. Regis 92.26 88 W. Paces Ferry Rd.; 877/787-3447; stregis.com. **$$**

Greensboro
ⓢ **Ritz-Carlton Lodge, Reynolds Plantation** 87.59 800/241-3333; ritzcarlton.com. **$$**

Savannah
ⓢ **Andaz (formerly the Avia)** 90.67 14 Barnard St.; 877/875-5036; aviahotels.com. **$**

ⓢ **Bohemian Hotel Savannah Riverfront** 87.62 102 W. Bay St.; 888/213-4024; bohemian hotelsavannah.com. **$**

ⓢ **Mansion on Forsyth Park** 88.67 700 Drayton St.; 888/213-3671; mansiononforsythpark.com. **$$**

Sea Island
Cloister at Sea Island 89.33 855/714-9201; seaisland.com. **$$$**

HAWAII
Big Island
Four Seasons Resort Hualalai 93.75 800/332-3442; fourseasons.com. **$$$$**

Hapuna Beach Prince Hotel 88.13 866/774-6236; princeresortshawaii.com. **$$$**

Mauna Kea Beach Hotel 87.58 877/880-6524; maunakeabeachhotel.com. **$$$$**

Mauna Lani Bay Hotel & Bungalows 89.05 800/367-2323; maunalani.com. **$$$**

Kauai
Grand Hyatt Kauai Resort & Spa 89.88 800/233-1234; hyatt.com. **$$$$**

Koa Kea Hotel & Resort 92.44 888/898-8958; koakea.com. **$$$**

St. Regis Princeville Resort 89.43 877/787-3447; stregis.com. **$$$$**

Lanai
Four Seasons Resort Lanai, The Lodge at Koele 92.32 800/332-3442; fourseasons.com. **$$$**

Maui
Fairmont Kea Lani 88.88 800/441-1414; fairmont.com. **$$$**

Four Seasons Resort Maui at Wailea 92.19 800/332-3442; fourseasons.com. **$$$$**

Ritz-Carlton, Kapalua 88.49 800/241-3333; ritzcarlton.com. **$$$$**

Oahu
Halekulani 91.05 800/367-2343; halekulani.com. **$$$**

Kahala Hotel & Resort 90.74 800/367-2525; kahalaresort.com. **$$$**

Royal Hawaiian, a Luxury Collection Resort 89.42 800/325-3589; royal-hawaiian.com. **$$$$**

ILLINOIS
Chicago
Four Seasons Hotel 90.33 120 E. Delaware Place; 800/332-3442; fourseasons.com. **$$$**

ⓢ **Park Hyatt** 90.04 800 N. Michigan Ave.; 877/875-4658; park.hyatt.com. **$$**

Peninsula Chicago 93.66 108 E. Superior St.; 866/382-8388; peninsula.com. **$$$**

Ritz-Carlton, Chicago, a Four Seasons Hotel 89.42 160 E. Pearson St.;

The Boulevard Pool
and cabanas at
the Cosmopolitan
of Las Vegas.

800/332-3442; fourseasons.com. $$

🅢 **Sofitel Chicago Water Tower** 88.10 20 E. Chestnut St.; 800/763-4835; sofitel.com. $

Trump International Hotel & Tower 90.00 401 N. Wabash Ave.; 855/878-6700; trumpchicagohotel.com. $$$

Waldorf Astoria 94.67 11 E. Walton St.; 800/925-3673; waldorfastoria.com. $$$

KENTUCKY
Louisville
21c Museum Hotel 89.39 700 W. Main St.; 877/217-6400; 21cmuseumhotels.com. $$

LOUISIANA
New Orleans
Ritz-Carlton 89.57 921 Canal St.; 800/241-3333; ritzcarlton.com. $$$

Roosevelt Hotel 90.04 123 Baronne St.; 800/925-3673; therooseveltneworleans.com. $$$

🅢 **Windsor Court Hotel** 89.03 300 Gravier St.; 800/262-2662; windsorcourthotel.com. $$

MAINE
Cape Elizabeth
Inn by the Sea 89.74 800/888-4287; innbythesea.com. $$

Rockport
Samoset Resort 88.09 800/341-1650; samoset.com. $$

MASSACHUSETTS
Boston
Boston Harbor Hotel at Rowes Wharf 90.30 70 Rowes Wharf; 800/752-7077; bhh.com. $$$$

Eliot Hotel 87.84 370 Commonwealth Ave.; 800/443-5468; eliothotel.com. $$

Four Seasons Hotel 90.45 200 Boylston St.; 800/332-3442; fourseasons.com. $$$

🅢 **Hotel Commonwealth** 89.09 500 Commonwealth Ave.;

866/784-4000; hotelcommonwealth.com. $$

Mandarin Oriental 91.17 776 Boylston St.; 800/526-6566; mandarinoriental.com. $$$

Ritz-Carlton, Boston Common 89.55 10 Avery St.; 800/241-3333; ritzcarlton.com. $$

XV Beacon 92.35 15 Beacon St.; 877/982-3226; xvbeacon.com. $$

Cape Cod
Chatham Bars Inn Resort & Spa 88.66 Chatham; 800/527-4884; chathambarsinn.com. $$

Wequassett Resort & Golf Club 92.57 Chatham; 800/225-7125; wequassett.com. $$$$

Martha's Vineyard
🅢 **Harbor View Hotel** 89.91 Edgartown; 800/225-6005; harbor-view.com. $

Nantucket
The Wauwinet 88.00 800/426-8718; wauwinet.com. $$

🅢 **White Elephant** 90.44 800/445-6574; whiteelephanthotel.com. $$

MINNESOTA
St. Paul
🅢 **Saint Paul Hotel** 87.87 350 Market St.; 800/292-9292; saintpaulhotel.com. $

MISSOURI
Kansas City
🅢 **Raphael Hotel** 87.82 325 Ward Pkwy.; 800/821-5342; raphaelkc.com. $

Ridgedale
🅢 **Big Cedar Lodge** 88.00 800/323-7500; bigcedar.com. $

St. Louis
Four Seasons Hotel 88.00 999 N. 2nd St.; 800/332-3442; fourseasons.com. $$

MONTANA
Darby
Triple Creek Ranch 98.22 800/654-2943;

triplecreekranch.com. $$$$

NEVADA
Las Vegas
🅢 **Bellagio Resort & Casino** 87.75 3600 Las Vegas Blvd. S.; 888/987-6667; bellagio.com. $

🅢 **Cosmopolitan of Las Vegas** 89.38 3708 Las Vegas Blvd. S.; 877/551-7778; cosmopolitanlasvegas.com. $

🅢 **Encore** 88.38 3131 Las Vegas Blvd. S.; 888/320-7125; encorelasvegas.com. $

🅢 **Four Seasons Hotel** 90.17 3960 Las Vegas Blvd. S.; 800/332-3442; fourseasons.com. $

Mandarin Oriental 91.86 3752 Las Vegas Blvd. S.; 800/526-6566; mandarinoriental.com. $$

🅢 **The Palazzo** 88.41 3325 Las Vegas Blvd. S.; 866/263-3001; palazzolasvegas.com. $

🅢 **The Venetian** 87.68 3355 Las Vegas Blvd. S.; 877/883-6423; venetian.com. $

🅢 **Wynn Las Vegas** 88.37 3131 Las Vegas Blvd. S.; 877/321-9966; wynnlasvegas.com. $

NEW HAMPSHIRE
New Castle
Wentworth by the Sea, a Marriott Hotel & Spa 90.93 888/252-6888; wentworth.com. $$

NEW MEXICO
Santa Fe Area
🅢 **Hyatt Regency Tamaya Resort & Spa** 88.82 Santa Ana Pueblo; 800/233-1234; hyatt.com. $$

Rosewood Inn of the Anasazi 90.22 Santa Fe; 888/767-3966; innoftheanasazi.com. $$

NEW YORK
Adirondacks
Friends Lake Inn 88.50 Chestertown;

518/494-4751; friendslake.com. $$

Lake Placid Lodge 88.39 Lake Placid; 877/523-2700; lakeplacidlodge.com. $$$$

Whiteface Lodge 88.36 Lake Placid; 800/903-4045; thewhitefacelodge.com. $$$

New York City
Andaz 5th Avenue 88.61 485 5th Ave.; 877/875-5036; andaz.com. $$$

Four Seasons Hotel 92.28 57 E. 57th St.; 800/332-3442; fourseasons.com. $$$$

Mandarin Oriental 89.27 80 Columbus Circle; 800/526-6566; mandarinoriental.com. $$$$

Peninsula New York 90.47 700 5th Ave.; 866/382-8388; peninsula.com. $$$$

The Pierre, a Taj Hotel 89.09 2 E. 61st St.; 866/969-1825; tajhotels.com. $$$$

Ritz-Carlton New York Central Park 91.14 50 Central Park S.; 800/241-3333; ritzcarlton.com. $$$$

Setai Fifth Avenue 88.84 400 5th Ave.; 877/247-6688; setaififthavenue.com. $$$$

St. Regis 87.93 2 E. 55th St.; 877/787-3447; stregis.com. $$$$$

The Surrey 88.46 20 E. 76th St.; 888/419-0052; thesurrey.com. $$$

Trump International Hotel & Tower 92.40 1 Central Park W.; 855/878-6700; trumpintl.com. $$$$

NORTH CAROLINA
Asheville
🅢 **Grand Bohemian Hotel** 89.57 888/717-8756; bohemianhotelasheville.com. $

Inn on Biltmore Estate 89.10 800/411-3812; biltmore.com. $$

Cary
Umstead Hotel & Spa 91.36 866/877-4141; theumstead.com. $$$

Charlotte
Ritz-Carlton 88.97 201 E. Trade St.; 800/241-3333; ritzcarlton.com. $$

Greensboro
Proximity Hotel 89.25 800/379-8200; proximityhotel.com. $$

Highlands
🅢 **Old Edwards Inn & Spa** 90.67 866/526-8008; oldedwardsinn.com. $$

Pinehurst
🅢 **Pinehurst Resort** 90.16 800/487-4653; pinehurst.com. $$

Pittsboro
Fearrington House Inn 89.14 800/277-0130; fearrington.com. $$

OREGON
Cannon Beach
Stephanie Inn Hotel 89.33 800/633-3466; stephanieinn.com. $$$

Gold Beach
🅢 **Tu Tu' Tun Lodge** 95.00 800/864-6357; tututun.com. $$

Newberg
Allison Inn & Spa 92.03 877/294-2525; theallison.com. $$

Portland
Heathman Hotel 89.04 1001 S.W. Broadway; 800/551-0011; heathmanhotel.com. $$

🅢 **The Nines, a Luxury Collection Hotel** 88.87 525 S.W. Morrison St.; 800/325-3589; thenines.com. $$

PENNSYLVANIA
Philadelphia
Four Seasons Hotel 88.96 1 Logan Square; 800/332-3442; fourseasons.com. $$

🅢 **Hotel Palomar** 89.00 117 S. 17th St.; 888/725-1778; hotelpalomar-philadelphia.com. $

🅢 **Rittenhouse Hotel** 90.07 210 W. Rittenhouse

KEY $ *Less than $200* $$ *$200 to $350* $$$ *$350 to $500* $$$$ *$500 to $1,000* $$$$$ *More than $1,000* 🅢 *Great Value ($250 or less)*

T+L 500

261

Square; 800/635-1042;
rittenhousehotel.com. **$$**

Ritz-Carlton 89.38
10 Ave. of the Arts;
800/241-3333;
ritzcarlton.com. **$$$**

RHODE ISLAND
Newport
Castle Hill 87.79
888/466-1355;
castlehillinn.com. **$$$$**

Chanler at Cliff Walk
89.14 888/552-2588;
thechanler.com. **$$$$**

Watch Hill
Ocean House 93.14
888/552-2588;
oceanhouseri.com. **$$$$**

SOUTH CAROLINA
Aiken
Ⓢ **The Willcox** 94.25
877/648-2200;
thewillcox.com. **$**

Bluffton
**Inn at Palmetto Bluff,
an Auberge Resort**
92.65 866/706-6565;
palmettobluff.com. **$$$**

Charleston
Ⓢ **Charleston Place**
89.59 205 Meeting St.;
888/635-2350;
charlestonplace.com. **$$**

Market Pavilion Hotel
91.79 225 E. Bay St.;
877/440-2250;
marketpavilion.com. **$$**

Planters Inn
88.84 112 N. Market St.;
800/845-7082;
plantersinn.com. **$$**

Wentworth Mansion
95.47 149 Wentworth St.;
888/466-1886; wentworth
mansion.com. **$$**

Kiawah Island
**Sanctuary at Kiawah
Island Golf Resort**
92.10 800/654-2924;
kiawahresort.com. **$$$**

TENNESSEE
Nashville
Hermitage Hotel 92.72
231 6th Ave. N.; 888/888-
9414; thehermitagehotel.
com. **$$**

Ⓢ **Hutton Hotel** 87.56
1808 West End Ave.;
615/340-9333;
huttonhotel.com. **$$**

Walland
Blackberry Farm 92.72
800/648-4252; blackberry
farm.com. **$$$$**

TEXAS
Dallas Area
**Four Seasons
Resort & Club Dallas at
Las Colinas** 90.74
4150 N. MacArthur Blvd.,
Irving; 800/332-3442;
fourseasons.com. **$$**

**The Joule, a Luxury
Collection Hotel** 87.83
1530 Main St., Dallas;
800/325-3589;
thejouledallas.com. **$$$**

Ritz-Carlton 88.08
2121 McKinney Ave.,
Dallas; 800/241-3333;
ritzcarlton.com. **$$$**

**Rosewood Crescent
Hotel** 87.91
400 Crescent Court,
Dallas; 888/767-3966;
crescentcourt.com. **$$**

**Rosewood Mansion
on Turtle Creek** 94.18
2821 Turtle Creek Blvd.,
Dallas; 888/767-3966;
mansiononturtlecreek.
com. **$$$**

San Antonio
Ⓢ **Hotel Valencia
Riverwalk** 88.52
150 E. Houston St.; 866/
842-0100; hotelvalencia-
riverwalk.com. **$$**

UTAH
Canyon Point
Amangiri 93.33 877/695-
3999; amangiri.com. **$$$$**

Park City
Montage Deer Valley
89.68 800/323-7500;
montagedeervalley.com.
$$$$

Stein Eriksen Lodge
91.60 800/453-1302;
steinlodge.com. **$$$**

St. Regis, Deer Valley
91.20 877/787-3447;
stregis.com. **$$$**

Waldorf Astoria 91.43
800/925-3673; waldorf
astoria.com. **$$$**

Salt Lake City
Grand America Hotel
88.35 555 S. Main St.;
800/621-4505;
grandamerica.com. **$$**

VIRGINIA
Alexandria
Ⓢ **Morrison House**
93.50 866/834-6628;
morrisonhouse.com. **$$**

Arlington
**Ritz-Carlton, Pentagon
City** 89.17 800/241-3333;
ritzcarlton.com. **$$$**

Charlottesville
Keswick Hall 90.00
800/274-5391;
keswick.com. **$$$**

Hot Springs
Ⓢ **Homestead Resort &
Spa** 88.00 800/838-1766;
thehomestead.com. **$$**

McLean
**Ritz-Carlton, Tysons
Corner** 87.87 800/241-
3333; ritzcarlton.com. **$$$**

Richmond
Ⓢ **Jefferson Hotel**
88.35 800/424-8014;
jeffersonhotel.com. **$$**

Washington
**Inn at Little
Washington** 90.94
540/675-3800; theinnat
littlewashington.com. **$$$**

Williamsburg
Williamsburg Inn 90.44
800/447-8679; colonial
williamsburg.com. **$$**

WASHINGTON
Seattle
Four Seasons Hotel
88.19 99 Union St.;
800/332-3442;
fourseasons.com. **$$$**

Ⓢ **Hotel 1000** 89.60
1000 1st Ave.; 877/315-1088;
hotel1000seattle.com. **$$**

Inn at the Market 88.76
86 Pine St.; 800/446-4484;
innatthemarket.com. **$$**

Snoqualmie
Ⓢ **Salish Lodge & Spa**
87.69 800/272-5474;
salishlodge.com. **$$**

WEST VIRGINIA
White Sulphur Springs
Ⓢ **The Greenbrier**
89.65 800/624-6070;
greenbrier.com. **$$**

WISCONSIN
Kohler
American Club Resort
88.23 800/344-2838;
americanclubresort.com. **$$**

WYOMING
Jackson Hole
Amangani 92.62
800/477-9180;
amangani.com. **$$$$**

Four Seasons Resort
90.36 800/332-3442;
fourseasons.com. **$$$**

Canada

ALBERTA
Banff
Rimrock Resort Hotel
88.15 888/746-7625;
rimrockresort.com. **$$$**

Lake Louise
**Fairmont Chateau Lake
Louise** 88.63 800/441-
1414; fairmont.com. **$$**

Post Hotel & Spa 89.93
800/661-1586;
posthotel.com. **$$**

BRITISH
COLUMBIA
Sooke
Ⓢ **Sooke Harbour
House** 90.80 800/889-
9688; sookeharbourhouse.
com. **$**

Tofino
Wickaninnish Inn 91.33
800/333-4604;
wickinn.com. **$$$**

Vancouver
Shangri-La Hotel 88.67
1128 W. Georgia St.;
866/565-5050;
shangri-la.com. **$$**

Whistler
**Fairmont Chateau
Whistler** 88.73
800/441-1414;
fairmont.com. **$$**

Four Seasons Resort
90.24 800/332-3442;
fourseasons.com. **$$**

ONTARIO
Toronto
Ritz-Carlton 89.58
181 Wellington St. W.;
800/241-3333;
ritzcarlton.com. **$$$**

QUEBEC
La Malbaie
Ⓢ **Fairmont Le
Manoir Richelieu** 88.00
800/441-1414;
fairmont.com. **$$**

Quebec City
Ⓢ **Auberge Saint-
Antoine** 93.12
8 Rue St.-Antoine;
888/692-2211;
saint-antoine.com. **$$**

The Caribbean, Bermuda + The Bahamas

BERMUDA
The Reefs 92.71
Southampton;
800/742-2008;
thereefs.com. **$$$$**

**Rosewood Tucker's
Point** 88.42 Hamilton
Parish; 888/767-3966;
rosewoodhotels.com.
$$$$

BRITISH VIRGIN
ISLANDS
Virgin Gorda
Biras Creek Resort
90.44 877/883-0756;
biras.com. **$$$**

CAYMAN ISLANDS
Grand Cayman
Ritz-Carlton 89.18
800/241-3333;
ritzcarlton.com. **$$$$**

JAMAICA
Couples Negril 90.36
Hanover; 800/268-7537
couples.com; all-inclusive;
3-night minimum. **$$$$**

Couples Sans Souci
90.84 St. Mary;
800/268-7537; couples.
com; all-inclusive;
3-night minimum. **$$$$**

Couples Swept Away
90.29 Westmoreland;
800/268-7537; couples.
com; all-inclusive;
3-night minimum. **$$$$**

Couples Tower Isle
90.71 St. Mary;
800/268-7537; couples.
com; all-inclusive;
3-night minimum. **$$$$**

PUERTO RICO
Vieques
W Retreat & Spa 87.85

The Presidential Suite at Virginia's Inn at Little Washington.

877/946-8357; whotels.com. $$$

NEVIS
Four Seasons Resort
88.14 Charlestown; 800/332-3442; fourseasons.com. $$$$

Nisbet Plantation Beach Club 92.00 St. James Parish; 800/742-6008; nisbetplantation.com. $$$$

ST. BART'S
Eden Rock 91.86 Baie de St.-Jean; 855/333-6762; edenrockhotel.com. $$$$

Hotel Saint Barth Isle de France 90.22 Baie des Flamands; 800/810-4691; isle-de-france.com. $$$$

ST. LUCIA
Jade Mountain 91.52 Soufrière; 800/223-1108; jademountain.com. $$$$$

TURKS AND CAICOS
Ocean Club Resorts 88.27 Providenciales; 800/457-8787; oceanclubresorts.com; $$

Regent Palms 88.95 Providenciales; 866/877-7256; regenthotels.com. $$$$

U.S. VIRGIN ISLANDS
St. Thomas
Ritz-Carlton 87.71 800/241-3333; ritzcarlton.com. $$$$

Mexico

Acapulco
🟢 **Fairmont Acapulco Princess** 89.76 Playa Revolcadero; 800/441-1414; fairmont.com. $$

Cancún
Live Aqua 94.22 Km 12.5, Blvd. Kukulkán;

800/343-7821; feel-aqua.com. $$$$

Ritz-Carlton 89.18 36 Retorno del Rey; 800/241-3333; ritzcarlton.com. $$$

Los Cabos
Capella Pedregal 93.29 San José del Cabo; 877/247-6688; capellahotels.com. $$$$

Esperanza, an Auberge Resort 88.90 Punta Ballena; 866/311-2226; esperanzaresort.com. $$$$

Las Ventanas al Paraíso, A Rosewood Resort 91.09 San José del Cabo; 888/767-3966; lasventanas.com. $$$$

One&Only Palmilla 91.14 San José del Cabo; 866/829-2977; oneandonly resorts.com. $$$$

Pueblo Bonito Pacifica Resort & Spa 87.61 Cabo San Lucas; 800/990-8250; pueblobonito pacifica.com. $$$

Secrets Marquis 87.78 San José del Cabo; 866/467-3273; secretsresorts.com. $$$$$

Mexico City
Four Seasons Hotel Mexico, D.F. 90.40 500 Paseo de la Reforma; 800/332-3442; fourseasons.com. $$$

Punta Mita
Four Seasons Resort 90.52 800/332-3442; fourseasons.com. $$$

St. Regis Punta Mita Resort 91.72 877/787-3447; stregis.com. $$$$$

Riviera Maya
Banyan Tree Mayakoba Resort & Spa 89.43 Solidaridad; 800/591-0439; banyantree.com. $$$$

Fairmont Mayakoba 88.00 Solidaridad; 800/441-1414; fairmont.com. $$$

Grand Velas 93.80 Solidaridad; 877/418-2963; grandvelas.com. $$$$

Iberostar Paraíso Maya Hotel 88.50 Solidaridad; 888/923-2722; iberostar. com; all-inclusive. $$$$

Royal Hideaway Playacar 88.71 Solidaridad; 800/999-9182; royalhideaway.com. $$$

Secrets Maroma Beach Riviera Cancún 90.47 Punta Maroma; 866/467-3273; secrets resorts.com. $$$$$

Puerto Vallarta Area
Grand Velas Riviera Nayarit 88.96 Nuevo Vallarta; 877/418-2722; grandvelas.com. $$$$

Zihuatanejo
La Casa Que Canta 93.20 888/523-5050; lacasaquecanta.com. $$$

Central + South America

ARGENTINA
Bariloche
Llao Llao Hotel & Resort, Golf-Spa 92.31

800/223-6800; llaollao.com.ar. $$$

Buenos Aires
Alvear Palace Hotel 90.05 1891 Avda. Alvear; 877/457-6315; alvearpalace.com. $$$$

Four Seasons Hotel 89.29 1086/88 Calle Posadas; 800/332-3442; fourseasons.com. $$$$

🟢 **InterContinental** 90.11 809 Moreno St.; 800/237-0200; intercontinental.com. $

Palacio Duhau - Park Hyatt 96.13 1661 Avda. Alvear; 877/875-4658; park.hyatt.com. $$$$

Mendoza
Park Hyatt 89.19 877/875-4658; park.hyatt.com. $$

BELIZE
San Ignacio
Lodge at Chaa Creek 88.24 877/709-8708; chaacreek.com. $$

CHILE
Santiago
Grand Hyatt 92.62 4601 Avda. Kennedy; 800/233-1234; grand.hyatt.com. $$

Ritz-Carlton 89.04 15 Calle El Alcalde; 800/241-3333; ritzcarlton.com. $$$

Torres del Paine National Park
Hotel Salto Chico/ Explora Patagonia 94.40 866/750-6699; explora.com; all-inclusive; 4-night minimum. $$$$$

COSTA RICA
Arenal Volcano National Park
🟢 **Nayara Hotel, Spa & Gardens** 96.36 La Fortuna; 866/311-1197; arenalnayara.com. $$

Guanacaste
Four Seasons Resort Costa Rica at Peninsula Papagayo 91.83 800/332-3442; fourseasons.com. $$$$

Playa Herradura
Los Sueños Marriott Ocean & Golf Resort 88.67 800/228-9290; marriott.com. $$$

L'Oustau de
Baumanière & Spa,
in Les Baux-de-
Provence, France.

GUATEMALA
Antigua
ⓢ **Hotel Museo Casa Santo Domingo** 92.67
502/7820-1222; casasanto domingo.com.gt. **$$**

PERU
Cuzco
Hotel Monasterio 90.15
136 Calle Palacio;
800/237-1236; monasterio hotel.com. **$$$$**

Lima
JW Marriott Lima Hotel 90.07 615 Malecón de la Reserva; 800/228-9290; marriott.com. **$$$**

Machu Picchu Pueblo
Inkaterra Machu Picchu Pueblo Hotel 91.63
800/442-5042;
inkaterra.com. **$$$**

Europe

AUSTRIA
Salzburg
Hotel Goldener Hirsch, a Luxury Collection Hotel 89.71
37 Getreidegasse;
800/325-3589;
goldenerhirsch.com. **$$**

Vienna
Hotel Bristol, a Luxury Collection Hotel
92.46 1 Kärntner Ring;
800/325-3589;
bristolvienna.com. **$$**

Hotel Imperial, a Luxury Collection Hotel
90.00 16 Kärntner Ring;
800/325-3589; hotel imperialvienna.com. **$$$**

Hotel Sacher Wien 89.54
4 Philharmonikerstrasse;
800/223-6800;
sacher.com. **$$$$**

BELGIUM
Brussels
Hotel Amigo 89.44
1-3 Rue de l'Amigo;
888/667-9477;
hotelamigo.com. **$$**

CZECH REPUBLIC
Prague
Four Seasons Hotel
89.37 2A/1098
Veleslavínova; 800/332-3442; fourseasons.com. **$$$**

ENGLAND
Bath
Royal Crescent Hotel
87.78 800/735-2478;
royalcrescent.co.uk. **$$$**

Berkshire
Cliveden House 89.33
Taplow; 44-1628/668-561;
clivedenhouse.co.uk. **$$$**

London
The Berkeley
90.14 Wilton Place;
866/599-6991;
the-berkeley.co.uk. **$$$$**

Chesterfield Mayfair
89.00 35 Charles St.;
877/955-1515; chesterfield mayfair.com. **$$**

Claridge's 88.00
49 Brook St.; 866/599-6991;
claridges.co.uk. **$$$$$**

The Dorchester, Dorchester Collection
88.70 Park Lane;
800/650-1842;
thedorchester.com. **$$$$**

41 88.14 41 Buckingham
Palace Rd.; 877/955-1515;
41hotel.com. **$$$**

Four Seasons Hotel London at Park Lane
91.68 Hamilton Place,
Park Lane; 800/332-3442;
fourseasons.com.
$$$$$

The Goring 87.53
Beeston Place;
800/608-0273;
thegoring.com. **$$$$**

The Lanesborough
90.82 Hyde Park Corner;
800/999-1828;
lanesborough.com. **$$$$**

Mandarin Oriental Hyde Park 89.33
66 Knightsbridge;
800/526-6566; mandarin oriental.com. **$$$$**

Milestone Hotel 92.83
1 Kensington Court;
800/223-6800; milestone hotel.com. **$$$**

The Savoy 89.36
Strand; 800/633-7575;
fairmont.com. **$$$$**

Soho Hotel 90.59
4 Richmond Mews;
44-20/7559-3000;
firmdale.com. **$$$**

Stafford London by Kempinski 91.47

St. James's Place; 800/426-3135; kempinski.com. **$$$**

FRANCE
Côte d'Azur
Hôtel Château Eza
89.33 Èze Village;
33-4/93-41-12-24;
chateaueza.com. **$$$**

Hôtel du Cap-Eden-Roc 89.20 Antibes;
33-4/93-61-39-01; hotel-du-cap-eden-roc.com. **$$$$$**

Le Palais de la Méditerranée 89.50
13 Promenade des Anglais,
Nice; 800/888-4747;
palais.concorde-hotels.
com. **$$$**

Onzain
Domaine des Hauts de Loire 93.00
800/735-2478; domaine hautsloire.com. **$$**

Paris
Four Seasons Hotel George V 91.58 31 Ave.
George V; 800/332-3442;
fourseasons.com. **$$$$$**

Hôtel de Crillon 90.67
10 Place de la Concorde;
800/888-4747;
crillon.com. **$$$$$**

Hôtel Plaza Athénée, Dorchester Collection
92.86 25 Ave. Montaigne;
800/650-1842;
plaza-athenee-paris.com.
$$$$$

Le Bristol 91.33 112 Rue
du Faubourg St.-Honoré;
800/745-8883;
lebristolparis.com.
$$$$$

Le Meurice, Dorchester Collection 90.83 228 Rue
de Rivoli; 800/650-1842;
lemeurice.com. **$$$$**

Park Hyatt Paris-Vendôme 88.16 5 Rue de
la Paix; 877/875-4658;
park.hyatt.com. **$$$$$**

The Ritz (closed for renovations until summer 2014) 89.21
15 Place Vendôme; 33-1/43-16-30-30; ritzparis.com.

Provence
Hôtel Crillon le Brave
93.05 Crillon-le-Brave;
800/735-2478;
crillonbrave.com. **$$$**

La Mirande 88.21
Avignon; 33-4/90-14-20-20;
la-mirande.fr. **$$$$**

L'Oustau de Baumanière & Spa
91.78 Les Baux-de-Provence; 33-4/90-54-33-07; oustaudebaumaniere.
com. **$$**

Villa Gallici 88.32
Aix-en-Provence;
800/735-2478;
villagallici.com. **$$$$**

Reims
Le Château Les Crayères 92.38
64 Blvd. Henry Vasnier;
800/735-2478;
lescrayeres.com. **$$$$**

GERMANY
Baden-Baden
Brenners Park-Hotel & Spa 89.47 49-7221/9000;
brenners.com. **$$$**

Berlin
Hotel Adlon Kempinski
90.50 77 Unter den
Linden; 800/426-3135;
hotel-adlon.de. **$$$**

Ritz-Carlton 90.11
3 Potsdamer Platz;
800/241-3333;
ritzcarlton.com. **$$**

Munich
Mandarin Oriental
90.00 1 Neuturmstrasse;
800/526-6566; mandarin oriental.com. **$$$$**

GREECE
Athens
Hotel Grande Bretagne, a Luxury Collection Hotel 88.62
A1 Vas. Georgiou St.;
800/325-3589;
grandebretagne.gr. **$$$**

King George Palace
89.09 3 Vas. Georgiou St.;
30-210/322-2210;
kinggeorgepalace.com.
$$

Santorini
Katikies Hotel 93.07
Oia; 30-22860/71401;
katikieshotelsantorini.
com. **$$$$**

Vedema, a Luxury Collection Resort 88.73
Megalohori; 800/325-3589;
vedema.gr. **$$$$**

HUNGARY
Budapest
Four Seasons Hotel Gresham Palace
93.50 5-6 Roosevelt Tér;
800/332-3442;
fourseasons.com. **$$**

ⓢ **InterContinental**
89.26 12-14 Apáczai Csere
János Ut.; 800/327-0200;
intercontinental.com. **$**

IRELAND
County Clare
Dromoland Castle
91.48 Newmarket on
Fergus; 800/346-7007;
dromoland.ie. **$$$**

Lodge at Doonbeg
93.56 Doonbeg;
866/366-6234;
doonbeglodge.com. **$$$**

County Kerry
Sheen Falls Lodge
93.40 Kenmare;
800/735-2478;
sheenfallslodge.ie. **$$$$**

County Kildare
Kildare Hotel, Spa & Country Club 90.40
Straffan; 800/323-7500;
kclub.ie. **$$$**

County Limerick
Adare Manor Hotel & Golf Resort 89.78
Adare; 800/462-3273;
adaremanor.com. **$$**

County Mayo
Ashford Castle 90.29
Cong; 800/346-7007;
ashford.ie. **$$$$**

County Wicklow
Ritz-Carlton Powerscourt 90.54
Enniskerry; 800/241-3333;
ritzcarlton.com. **$$$**

Dublin
ⓢ **Four Seasons Hotel**
89.33 Simmonscourt Rd.;
800/332-3442;
fourseasons.com. **$$**

Merrion Hotel 91.50
Upper Merrion St.;
800/223-6800;
merrionhotel.com. **$$$$**

The Shelbourne 90.20
27 St. Stephen's Green;
800/228-9290;
marriott.com. **$$**

ITALY
Amalfi Coast
Hotel Caruso 93.25

Ravello; 800/237-1236; hotelcaruso.com. **$$$$**

Hotel Santa Caterina 94.48 Amalfi; 800/223-6800; hotelsantacaterina. it. **$$$$**

Il San Pietro di Positano 91.47 800/735 2478; ilsanpietro.it. **$$$$**

Le Sirenuse 93.33 Positano; 800/223-6800; sirenuse.it. **$$$$**

Palazzo Avino (formerly Palazzo Sasso) 93.64 Ravello; 39-089/818-181; palazzoavino.com. **$$$**

Capri
Grand Hotel Quisisana 88.71 800/223-6800; quisisana.com. **$$$**

Hotel Caesar Augustus 90.50 39-081/837-3395; caesar-augustus.com. **$$$$**

Florence
Four Seasons Hotel Firenze 91.75 99 Borgo Pinti; 800/332-3442; fourseasons.com. **$$$**

Hotel Lungarno 88.00 14 Borgo San Jacopo; 39-055/2726-4000; lungarnocollection.com. **$$**

St. Regis 89.60 1 Piazza d'Ognissanti; 877/787-3447; stregis.com. **$$$**

Lake Como
Grand Hotel Villa Serbelloni 89.58 Bellagio; 800/860-8672; villaserbelloni.com. **$$$$**

Villa d'Este 91.61 Cernobbio; 800/223-6800; villadeste.com. **$$$$**

Milan
Four Seasons Hotel Milano 92.00 6/8 Via Gesù; 800/332-3442; fourseasons.com. **$$$$$**

Hotel Principe di Savoia, Dorchester Collection 87.48 17 Piazza della Repubblica; 800/650-1842; hotelprincipedisavoia. com. **$$$**

Park Hyatt 89.57 1 Via Tommaso Grossi;

877/875-4658; park.hyatt. com. **$$$$**

Portofino
Hotel Splendido 91.37 800/237-1236; hotel splendido.com. **$$$$$**

Rome
Hotel Hassler Roma 89.33 6 Piazza Trinità dei Monti; 800/223-6800; hotel hasslerroma.com. **$$$**

Sorrento
Grand Hotel Excelsior Vittoria 88.94 800/325-8541; exvitt.it. **$$$$**

Taormina
Grand Hotel Timeo by Orient-Express 88.70 800/237-1236; grandhotel timeo.com. **$$$$**

Venice
Bauers Il Palazzo 89.13 1459 San Marco; 800/223-6800; ilpalazzo venezia.com. **$$$$**

ⓢ **Ca' Sagredo Hotel** 90.60 4198/99 Campo Santa Sofia; 800/525-4800; casagredohotel.com. **$$**

Hotel Cipriani 87.55 10 Giudecca; 800/237-1236; hotelcipriani.com. **$$$$$**

MONACO
Monte Carlo
Fairmont 87.74 12 Ave. des Spélugues; 800/441-1414; fairmont.com. **$$$**

Hôtel de Paris 91.36 Place du Casino; 800/595-0898; hoteldeparis montecarlo.com. **$$$$**

Hôtel Hermitage 91.75 Place Beaumarchais; 800/595-0898; hotelhermitagemontecarlo. com. **$$$**

POLAND
Warsaw
ⓢ **Le Méridien Bristol** 91.53 42-44 Krakowskie Przedmiescie; 800/543-4300; lemeridien.com. **$**

PORTUGAL
Lisbon
Four Seasons Hotel Ritz 92.12 88 Rua Rodrigo da Fonseca; 800/332-3442; fourseasons.com. **$$$$**

Olissippo Lapa Palace 90.95 4 Rua do Pau de Bandeira; 800/233-6800; olissippohotels.com. **$$$**

RUSSIA
Moscow
Ritz-Carlton 91.56 3 Tverskaya Ul.; 800/241-3333; ritzcarlton.com. **$$$**

St. Petersburg
Grand Hotel Europe 89.04 1/7 Mikhailovskaya Ul.; 800/237-1236; grandhoteleurope.com. **$$$$**

SCOTLAND
St. Andrews
Old Course Hotel, Golf Resort & Spa 87.52 800/223-6800; oldcoursehotel.co.uk. **$$**

SPAIN
Barcelona
Hotel Arts 90.67 19-21 Carrer de la Marina; 800/241-3333; ritzcarlton.com. **$$$**

Madrid
Hotel Ritz 90.12 5 Plaza de la Lealtad; 800/237-1236; ritzmadrid.com. **$$$**

ⓢ **InterContinental** 90.22 49 Paseo de la Castellana; 800/327-0200; intercontinental.com. **$$**

Seville
Hotel Alfonso XIII, a Luxury Collection Resort 88.48 2 Calle San Fernando; 800/325-3589; hotel-alfonsoxiii-seville. com. **$$**

SWEDEN
Stockholm
Grand Hôtel 88.12 8 Södra Blasieholms-hamnen; 800/327-0200; grandhotel.se. **$$$**

SWITZERLAND
Interlaken
Victoria-Jungfrau Grand Hotel & Spa 88.00 800/223-6800; victoria-jungfrau.ch. **$$**

Zurich
Baur au Lac 90.95 1 Talstrasse; 800/223-6800; bauraulac.ch. **$$$$**

TURKEY
Istanbul
Çırağan Palace Kempinski 90.53 32 Çırağan Cad.; 800/426-3135; kempinski.com. **$$$**

Four Seasons Hotel Istanbul at Sultanahmet 93.36 1 Tevkifhane Sk.; 800/332-3442; four seasons.com. **$$$**

Four Seasons Hotel Istanbul at the Bosphorus 94.54 28 Çırağan Cad.; 800/332-3442; fourseasons.com. **$$$**

Grand Hyatt Istanbul 91.11 1 Taskisla Cad.; 800/233-1234; grand.hyatt.com. **$$**

Africa +The Middle East

BOTSWANA
Moremi Game Reserve
Mombo Camp and Little Mombo Camp 95.17 27-11/807-1800; wilderness-safaris.com; all-inclusive. **$$$$$**

EGYPT
Cairo
Four Seasons Hotel Cairo at Nile Plaza 90.49 1089 Corniche El Nil; 800/332-3442; fourseasons.com. **$$**

Four Seasons Hotel Cairo at the First Residence 91.64 35 El Giza St.; 800/332-3442; fourseasons.com. **$$**

Mena House Oberoi 91.27 Pyramids Rd.; 800/562-3764; oberoihotels.com. **$$$**

ISRAEL
Jerusalem
King David Hotel 88.00 23 King David St.; 800/223-7773; danhotels.com. **$$$$**

JORDAN
Dead Sea
Kempinski Hotel Ishtar 87.60 Swaimeh; 800/426-3135; kempinski.com. **$$$**

KENYA
Amboseli National Park
Amboseli Serena Safari Lodge 88.83 254-20/284-2333; serenahotels.com; meals included. **$$$**

Tortilis Camp 92.40 254-20/600-3090; tortilis. com; all-inclusive. **$$$$**

Masai Mara
National Reserve
andBeyond Kichwa Tembo 94.48 27-11/809-4441; andbeyond.com; all-inclusive. **$$$$**

Fairmont Mara Safari Club 94.84 800/441-1414; fairmont.com; meals included. **$$$$**

Mara Serena Safari Lodge 88.00 254-20/284-2333; serenahotels.com; meals included. **$$$$**

Nairobi Area
Fairmont The Norfolk 89.06 Harry Thuku Rd.; 800/441-1414; fairmont.com. **$$**

Giraffe Manor 91.53 Koitobos Rd.; 254-20/502-0888; giraffemanor.com; meals included. **$$$$**

Nanyuki
Fairmont Mount Kenya Safari Club 93.60 800/441-1414; fairmont.com; meals included. **$$$$**

MOROCCO
Marrakesh
La Mamounia 90.52 Ave. Bab Jdid; 800/223-6800; mamounia.com. **$$$$**

SOUTH AFRICA
Cape Town
Cape Grace 93.65 W. Quay Rd.; 800/223-6800; capegrace.com. **$$$$**

Mount Nelson Hotel 90.20 76 Orange St.; 800/237-1236; mountnelson.co.za. **$$**

KEY **$** *Less than $200* **$$** *$200 to $350* **$$$** *$350 to $500* **$$$$** *$500 to $1,000* **$$$$$** *More than $1,000* ⓢ *Great Value ($250 or less)*

The 85th-floor swimming pool at the Park Hyatt Shanghai.

One&Only 95.33
Dock Rd.; 866/552-0001;
oneandonlyresorts.com.
$$$$

**Twelve Apostles
Hotel & Spa**
93.71 Victoria Rd.;
800/223-6800; 12apostles
hotel.com. **$$$$**

Victoria & Alfred Hotel
88.16 Dock Rd.; 27-21/419-
6677; vahotel.co.za. **$$$**

Franschhoek
Le Quartier Français
89.42 800/735-2478;
lqf.co.za. **$$$**

Johannesburg
**Saxon Boutique
Hotel, Villas & Spa**
94.22 36 Saxon Rd.;
27-11/292-6000;
saxon.co.za. **$$$$**

The Westcliff 89.55
67 Jan Smuts Ave.;
800/237-1236; westcliff.
co.za. **$$**

Kruger National
Park Area
**MalaMala Game
Reserve** 89.27

27-13/735-9200; malamala.
com; meals included.
$$$$$

**Sabi Sabi Private Game
Reserve Lodges** 95.40
Sabi Sand Reserve;
27-11/447-7172; sabisabi.
com; all-inclusive.
$$$$$

**Singita Kruger National
Park** 96.33 27-21/683-
3424; singita.com;
all-inclusive. **$$$$$**

Singita Sabi Sand
95.74 Sabi Sand Reserve;
27-21/683-3424;
singita.com; all-inclusive.
$$$$$

TANZANIA
Ngorongoro Crater
**andBeyond Ngorongoro
Crater Lodge**
92.88 27-11/809-4441;
andbeyond.com;
all-inclusive. **$$$$$**

**Ngorongoro Sopa
Lodge** 95.85
800/806-9565; sopalodges.
com; meals included. **$$$**

Serengeti National Park
**Kirawira Luxury
Tented Camp** 95.27
255-28/262-1518;
serenahotels.com.
$$$$

**Serengeti Sopa
Lodge** 92.89
800/806-9565
sopalodges.com;
meals included. **$$$**

Singita Grumeti
98.25 27-21/683-3424;
singita.com;
all-inclusive. **$$$$$**

**UNITED ARAB
EMIRATES**
Dubai
Burj Al Arab 89.82
Jumeirah; 877/854-8051;
jumeirah.com.
$$$$$

ZAMBIA
Livingstone
Royal Livingstone
89.90 260-21/332-1122;
suninternational.com.
$$$$

Asia

BHUTAN
Paro
Uma Paro 87.53
975-8/271-597;
uma.paro.como.bz. **$$$**

CAMBODIA
Siem Reap
Amansara 93.78 Road
to Angkor; 800/477-9180;
amanresorts.com.
$$$$

La Résidence d'Angkor
90.10 River Rd.;
855-63/963-390; residence
dangkor.com. **$$**

**Park Hyatt (formerly
Hôtel de la Paix)**
88.69 Sivutha Blvd.;
877/875-4658;
hoteldelapaixangkor.com.
$$$

**Raffles Grand Hotel
d'Angkor** 87.56
1 Vithei Charles de Gaulle;
800/768-9009;
raffles.com. **$$$**

**Sofitel Angkor
Phokeethra Golf &
Spa Resort** 92.86
Vithei Charles de Gaulle;
800/763-4835;
sofitel.com. **$$**

CHINA
Beijing
Peninsula Beijing 91.64
8 Goldfish Lane;
866/382-8388;
peninsula.com. **$$$$**

Ritz-Carlton 87.80
83A Jian Guo Rd.;
800/241-3333;
ritzcarlton.com. **$$$**

**Ritz-Carlton, Financial
Street** 91.25 1 Jin Cheng
Fang St. E., Financial St.;
800/241-3333;
ritzcarlton.com. **$$$$**

Hong Kong
Four Seasons Hotel
91.12 International
Finance Centre,
8 Finance St.; 800/332-
3442; fourseasons.com.
$$$$

InterContinental 89.38
18 Salisbury Rd.;
800/327-0200;
intercontinental.com.
$$$

Island Shangri-La
89.25 Pacific Place,
Supreme Court Rd.;

866/565-5050;
shangri-la.com. **$$$$**

Kowloon Shangri-La
88.43 64 Mody Rd.;
866/565-5050;
shangri-la.com. **$$$**

**Landmark Mandarin
Oriental** 89.50
15 Queen's Rd.; 800/526-
6566; mandarinoriental.
com. **$$$$**

Mandarin Oriental
91.66 5 Connaught Rd.;
800/526-6566; mandarin
oriental.com. **$$$$**

Peninsula Hong Kong
94.34 Salisbury Rd.;
866/382-8388;
peninsula.com. **$$$$**

Ritz-Carlton 89.00
International Commerce
Centre, 1 Austin Rd. W.;
800/241-3333;
ritzcarlton.com. **$$$$**

Shanghai
Park Hyatt 89.22
100 Century Ave.;
877/875-4658;
park.hyatt.com. **$$$**

Peninsula Shanghai
94.63 32 Zhongshan
Dong Yi Rd.; 866/382-8388;
peninsula.com. **$$$**

Pudong Shangri-La
90.40 33 Fu Cheng Rd.;
866/565-5050;
shangri-la.com. **$$**

INDIA
Agra
Oberoi Amarvilas
93.56 Taj E. Gate Rd.;
800/562-3764;
oberoihotels.com. **$$$$**

Bangalore
Leela Palace 90.11
23 Airport Rd.; 800/
426-3135; theleela.com. **$$**

Jaipur
Oberoi Rajvilas 94.45
Goner Rd.; 800/562-3764;
oberoihotels.com. **$$$$**

Rambagh Palace 93.00
Bhawani Singh Rd.;
866/969-1825;
tajhotels.com. **$$$**

Jodhpur
Umaid Bhawan Palace
94.07 Circuit House Rd.;
866/969-1825;
tajhotels.com. **$$$$**

Mumbai
Taj Mahal Palace
91.53 Apollo Bunder;

Overwater villas at
the Four Seasons
Resort Bora Bora, in
French Polynesia.

866/969-1825;
tajhotels.com. **$$$**

ⓢ **The Oberoi** 90.00
Sir Dorab Tata Rd.,
Nariman Point;
800/562-3764;
oberoihotels.com. **$$**

New Delhi
The Imperial 88.46
1 Janpath; 800/323-7500;
theimperialindia.com. **$$**

The Oberoi 88.12
Dr. Zakir Hussain Marg;
800/562-3764;
oberoihotels.com. **$$$**

Taj Mahal Hotel 92.00
1 Mansingh Rd.;
866/969-1825;
tajhotels.com. **$$**

ⓢ **Taj Palace Hotel**
89.09 Sardar Patel Marg,
Diplomatic Enclave;
866/969-1825;
tajhotels.com. **$**

Udaipur
Oberoi Udaivilas 97.50
Haridasji Ki Magri;
800/562-3764;
oberoihotels.com. **$$$$**

Taj Lake Palace 92.92 Lake Pichola;
866/969-1825;
tajhotels.com. **$$$$**

INDONESIA
Bali
ⓢ **Ayana Resort & Spa**
88.80 Jalan Karang Mas
Sejahtera; 62-361/702-222;
ayanaresort.com. **$$**

**Four Seasons Resort
Bali at Jimbaran Bay**
89.47 Jimbaran;
800/332-3442;
fourseasons.com. **$$$$**

JAPAN
Kyoto
ⓢ **Hyatt Regency** 88.13
644-2 Sanjusangendo-
mawari, Higashiyama-ku;
800/233-1234; hyatt.com.
$$

Tokyo
Grand Hyatt 90.35
6-10-3 Roppongi;
800/233-1234;
hyatt.com. **$$$$**

Mandarin Oriental
89.33 2-1-1 Nihonbashi
Muromachi; 800/526-
6566; mandarinoriental.
com. **$$$$**

Park Hyatt 91.16
Shinjuku Park Tower,
3-7-1-2 Nishi-Shinjuku;
877/875-4658;
park.hyatt.com. **$$$$**

Peninsula Tokyo
89.91 1-8-1 Yuraku-cho;
866/382-8388;
peninsula.com. **$$$$**

LAOS
Luang Prabang
La Résidence Phou Vao
92.80 800/237-1236;
residencephouvao.com.
$$$

MALAYSIA
Kuala Lumpur
ⓢ **Ritz-Carlton** 91.20
168 Jalan Imbi; 800/241-
3333; ritzcarlton.com. **$**

PHILIPPINES
Boracay
Discovery Shores 96.77
63-36/288-4500; discovery
shoresboracay.com. **$$**

Manila
ⓢ **Edsa Shangri-La**
88.00 1 Garden Way;
866/565-5050;
shangri-la.com. **$**

Makati Shangri-La
88.97 Ayala Ave. and
Makati Ave., Makati City;
866/565-5050;
shangri-la.com. **$$**

Peninsula Manila 88.00
Ayala and Makati Aves.;
866/382-8388;
peninsula.com. **$$$**

SINGAPORE
Capella
93.85 1 The Knolls;
800/223-6800;
capellahotels.com. **$$$$**

Conrad Centennial
88.29 2 Temasek Blvd.;
800/266-7237;
conradhotels.com. **$$**

Four Seasons Hotel
89.25 190 Orchard Blvd.;
800/332-3442;
fourseasons.com. **$$**

Fullerton Bay Hotel
88.21 80 Collyer Quay;
65/6333-8388; fullerton
bayhotel.com. **$$$**

Fullerton Hotel 89.74
1 Fullerton Square;
65/6733-8388;
fullertonhotel.com. **$$**

Mandarin Oriental
89.53 5 Raffles Ave.;
800/526-6566;
mandarinoriental.com.
$$$

Raffles Hotel 91.42
1 Beach Rd.; 800/768-9009;
raffleshotel.com.
$$$$$

Ritz-Carlton, Millenia
92.75 7 Raffles Ave.;
800/241-3333; ritzcarlton.
com. **$$$$**

Shangri-La Hotel 91.14
22 Orange Grove Rd.;
866/565-5050;
shangri-la.com. **$$$**

SOUTH KOREA
Seoul
Park Hyatt 88.00
606 Teheran-ro,
Gangnam-gu;
877/875-4658;
park.hyatt.com. **$$$**

The Shilla 91.16
202 Jangchung-dong
2-ga, Jung-gu;
800/223-6800; shilla.net.

THAILAND
Bangkok
ⓢ **Grand Hyatt Erawan**
90.46 494 Rajdamri Rd.;
800/233-1234; hyatt.com.
$$

ⓢ **JW Marriott** 88.00
4 Sukhumvit Rd., Soi 2;
800/228-9290;
jwmarriott.com. **$$**

Lebua at State Tower
89.41 1055 Silom Rd.;
66-2/624-9999;
lebua.com. **$$$**

Mandarin Oriental
95.04 48 Oriental Ave.;
800/526-6566; mandarin
oriental.com. **$$$**

Peninsula Bangkok
95.72 333 Charoennakorn
Rd.; 866/382-8388;
peninsula.com. **$$$**

ⓢ **Royal Orchid
Sheraton Hotel &
Towers** 90.78
2 Charoen Krung Rd.,
Soi 30; 800/325-3535;
sheraton.com. **$$**

ⓢ **Shangri-La Hotel**
90.42 89 Soi Wat
Suan Plu, New Rd.;
866/565-5050;
shangri-la.com. **$$**

The Sukhothai 90.35
13/3 S. Sathorn Rd.;
800/526-6566;
sukhothai.com. **$$$**

Chiang Mai
Four Seasons Resort
92.68 Mae Rim-Samoeng
Old Rd.; 800/332-3442;
fourseasons.com.
$$$$

ⓢ **Le Méridien,
Chiang Mai Resort**
87.69 108 Chang Klan Rd.;
800/543-4300;
lemeridien.com. **$**

**Mandarin Oriental
Dhara Dhevi** 92.38
51/4 Sankampaeng Rd.,
Moo 1; 800/526-6566;
mandarinoriental.com.
$$$$

Chiang Rai
**Anantara Golden
Triangle Resort & Spa**
88.80 Chiang Saen;
800/525-4800;
anantara.com. **$$$$$**

VIETNAM
Hanoi
ⓢ **Sofitel Legend
Metropole** 91.84
15 Ngo Quyen St.;
800/763-4835;
sofitel.com. **$$**

Ho Chi Minh City
Park Hyatt Saigon
92.62 2 Lam Son Square;
877/875-4658;
park.hyatt.com. **$$**

Hoi An
Nam Hai 87.79
84-51/394-0000;
thenamhai.com. **$$$$**

Australia, New Zealand + The South Pacific

AUSTRALIA
Great Barrier Reef
Hayman 89.00
Hayman Island;
800/745-8883;
hayman.com.au. **$$$$**

Lizard Island 94.53
61-3/9426-7550;

lizardisland.com.au;
meals included.
$$$$$

Kangaroo Island
Southern Ocean Lodge
97.87 61-2/9918-4355;
southernoceanlodge.com.
au; all-inclusive;
2-night minimum. **$$$$$**

Melbourne
The Langham
90.55 1 Southgate Ave.;
800/588-9141;
langhamhotels.com. **$$**

Sydney
Park Hyatt 88.20 7 Hickson Rd.;
877/875-4658;
park.hyatt.com. **$$$$**

Shangri-La Hotel
88.83 176 Cumberland St.;
866/565-5050;
shangri-la.com. **$$$**

**FRENCH
POLYNESIA**
Bora-Bora
Four Seasons Resort
93.68 Motu Tehotu;
800/332-3442;
fourseasons.com.
$$$$

St. Regis Resort
91.25 Motu Omee;
877/787-3447;
stregis.com. **$$$$$**

NEW ZEALAND
Christchurch
The George 87.77
50 Park Terrace;
64-3/371-0251;
thegeorge.com. **$$$**

Matauri Bay
Lodge at Kauri Cliffs
95.25 800/735-2478;
kauricliffs.com;
all-inclusive. **$$$$**

Taupo
Huka Lodge 93.50 800/735-2478;
hukalodge.com;
all-inclusive. **$$$$$**

Looking out over
the Valle de Guadalupe
from a balcony
at Mexico's Endémico
Resguardo Silvestre.

Trips Directory

Jerk-chicken spring rolls and conch fritters at Round Hill, in Jamaica.

Index

A guest bathroom at c/o The Maidstone, in the Hamptons, New York.

Contributors

Julian Allason

Richard Alleman

Aimee Lee Ball

Colin Barraclough

Thomas Beller

Kate Betts

Laura Begley Bloom

Rocky Casale

Jennifer Chen

Lisa Cheng

Chandrahas Choudhury

Colleen Clark

Stephen Drucker

Jonathan Durbin

Robyn Eckhardt

Sherri Eisenberg

Nikki Ekstein

Mark Ellwood

Amy Farley

Jennifer Flowers

Jaime Gillin

Lisa Grainger

Michael Gross

Chris Haslam

Farhad Heydari

Frances Hibbard

Tina Isaac

Karrie Jacobs

David Kaufman

David A. Keeps

Sarah Khan

Matt Lee

Ted Lee

Sharon Leece

Peter Jon Lindberg

Heather Smith MacIsaac

Alexandra Marshall

Andrew McCarthy

Meghan McEwen

Mario R. Mercado

Elizabeth Minchilli

Shane Mitchell

Bob Morris

Ian Mount

Lindsey Olander

Kathryn O'Shea-Evans

Brooke Porter

Josh Pramis

Ramsey Qubein

Kevin Raub

Sophy Roberts

Roxana Robinson

Maria Shollenbarger

Sarah Spagnolo

Scott Spencer

David Swanson

Laura Teusink

Suzanne Wales

Valerie Waterhouse

Peter Webster

Gisela Williams

Christian Lacroix–
designed uniforms on
the staff at the
Sofitel So Bangkok.

Photographers

Rainy-day diversions at Costa Rica's Oxygen Jungle Villas.